MEN HARVESTING WISDOM

MEN HARVESTING WISDOM. Copyright ©2026 by J. H. Parker.

All rights reserved. Printed in the United States of America. No part of this book may be used or reproduced in any manner whatsoever without written permission except in the case of brief quotations embodied in critical articles and reviews.

This book is designed to provide competent and reliable information regarding the subject matter covered. It is sold with the understanding that the author and publisher are not engaged in rendering professional psychological, medical, legal, or other professional services. If expert assistance is required, the services of a competent professional should be sought. The author and publisher specifically disclaim all responsibility for any liability, loss, or risk, personal or otherwise, that is incurred as a consequence, directly or indirectly, of the use and application of any of the contents of this book.

The stories and experiences shared in this book are true. Some names and identifying details have been changed to protect the privacy of individuals.

Without in any way limiting the author's [and publisher's] exclusive rights under copyright, any use of this publication to "train" generative artificial intelligence (AI) technologies to generate text is expressly prohibited. The author reserves all rights to license uses of this work for generative AI training and development of machine learning language models. This book may be purchased in bulk for promotional, educational, or business use. Please visit www.menharvestingwisdom.com.

Cover, graphics, and interior-layout design by Mariano Paniello.

ISBN: 978-0-9997-463-4-9 (paperback)

ISBN: 978-0-9997-463-3-2 (e-book)

ISBN: 978-0-9997-463-2-5 (hardcover)

Library of Congress Control Number: 2026901802

FIRST EDITION 2026

Advance Praise for
Men Harvesting Wisdom
by J. H. Parker

After reading hundreds of self-help books over the past five years, it takes something truly special to stand out. *Men Harvesting Wisdom* does exactly that— it stands out in the best possible way.

What sets this book apart is its universal approach to guiding readers through their own hero's journey. Many self-help books offer thought-provoking insights or the author's wisdom to solve a specific problem or improve one area of life. While helpful, those books often leave the reader to translate the advice and fit it into their broader personal journey. Parker's work goes deeper. Instead of simply offering answers, Men Harvesting Wisdom provides a clear roadmap and a practical workbook that empowers readers to look inward and discover their own solutions.

The value of this book depends largely on the reader's commitment. It does not promise quick fixes. Instead, it identifies specific actions and reflective practices that allow the reader— the hero of the story—to become who they are meant to be. In that sense, the book is less about consuming information and more about engaging in transformation.

Some books are meant to be read once or twice and then shared with others. This is not one of them. Men Harvesting Wisdom is a book I will return to regularly, using it as a personal compass. I can already imagine my copy filled with notes, worn pages, and insights collected over time. One day, my version of this book will be passed on to those I love, carrying not just Parker's wisdom, but my own journey within it.

Until then, I highly recommend *Men Harvesting Wisdom* to anyone seeking meaningful self-leadership. **The 10 Heroic Dimensions of Transformational Self-Leadership** offer a powerful framework for navigating life with intention, purpose, and courage. This is not just a book to read—it is a guide to live by.

— ***Clint,** Houston, Texas*

DISCLAIMER

The content in *Men Harvesting Wisdom: The Ten Heroic Dimensions of Transformational Self-Leadership* is intended for educational and informational purposes only. This book is not a substitute for professional mental health treatment, therapy, counseling, or medical advice.

If you are experiencing emotional distress or mental health challenges, please seek the guidance of a licensed mental health professional.

If you are in crisis, please call 911 immediately.

If you are a veteran in crisis, please contact the Veterans Crisis Line:

- Call: 988, then press 1
- Text: 838255
- Chat: VeteransCrisisLine.net

You are not alone. Help is available.

MEN HARVESTING WISDOM

The Ten Heroic Dimensions of Transformational Self-Leadership

A Field Guide for Managing Growth, Change, and Transition

By J.H. Parker

CONTENTS

Men Harvesting Wisdom i

Dedication iii

Introduction: **Why the Ten Heroic Dimensions Exist** 1

The First Heroic Dimension: **Identity** 23

The Second Heroic Dimension: **Values** 43

The Third Heroic Dimension: **Meaning** 59

The Fourth Heroic Dimension: **Purpose** 73

The Fifth Heroic Dimension: **Self-Care** 91

The Sixth Heroic Dimension: **Roles** 111

The Seventh Heroic Dimension: **Vision** 129

The Eighth Heroic Dimension: **Execution** 149

The Ninth Heroic Dimension: **Willingness** 171

The Tenth Heroic Dimension: **Legacy** 191

Triangulation for Managing Change and Transition: 209

Conclusion: 229

Afterword: 233

J. H. Parker 239

MEN HARVESTING WISDOM

If you are new to Men's Work, welcome.

Wherever you are, seek out Men's Work that resonates with you and join the campfire.

Men's Work is everywhere once you seek it.

If you are well traveled in Men's Work and leading others, welcome.

We have much to learn from one another as we harvest and share our collective wisdom.

Together, regardless of who we are, where we are from, our pasts, our differences, our beliefs, or faiths, we are honor-bound men from many backgrounds and wisdom traditions, creating space for our shared humanity.

For over three decades, my mission has been simple:

Save lives. Help men thrive. Keep families together.

The aim of this work is to help you discover and live your life with a profound realization:

Regardless of what you have been through, no matter how difficult, traumatizing, or heartbreaking, you have a deeper purpose to fulfill, and you deserve to live a fulfilling life.

And as you hold this realization for long enough, my hope is that you come to a second realization:

You deserve to be happy.

This work is a field guide for finding what we are all seeking:

Passionate – Sustainable – Clarity

"The meaning of life is to find your gift. The purpose of life is to give it away."
—Pablo Picasso

DEDICATION

For my son Danny, whose struggle to rebuild his life after military service inspired this work of helping people deal with change and transition while overcoming and transcending their past.

After leaving the Army, parts of Danny never fully came home—he left Afghanistan, but he couldn't outrun his demons from the war within.

The foundation for *Men Harvesting Wisdom* and *The Ten Heroic Dimensions of Transformational Self-Leadership* first began to emerge in 2004, from late-night phone calls with Danny about his struggles during a frozen East Coast winter when he first returned home.

Tragically, in 2009, Danny died in a high-speed, adrenaline-seeking motorcycle accident.

"Death ain't gonna touch you in your heart. It's just gonna come on up. It's just gonna walk on in and knock you down."
—Otis Taylor, *Live Your Life*

Losing Danny all but broke me. In his memory and to fill the void he had left, I became a wounded healer, desperately trying to shepherd others to safety. If I didn't move my pain, it would eat me alive.

Over time, sitting with countless Veterans and non-Veterans—men and women in their darkest moments of change and transition—and writing about what I've learned has allowed my grief to mature into something more than an unbearable raw wound. It has become wisdom. Not the kind that eliminates pain, but the kind that gives pain purpose.

Healing has no destination. It's an ongoing practice. But sometimes, lying on the ground broken open, you discover a purpose and strength you couldn't see when you were standing upright.

It is a brutal paradox to miss Danny so deeply while carrying profound gratitude for what losing him made me become.

This journey of guiding and supporting others through the same darkness I have been through has become my purpose.

All that is asked of you in this work is to harvest the wisdom from your journey and pay it forward to others.

This work is dedicated to Danny's legacy and to every person who carries invisible wounds.

INTRODUCTION:

WHY THE TEN HEROIC DIMENSIONS EXIST

"In times of change, learners inherit the earth, while the learned find themselves beautifully equipped to deal with a world that no longer exists."

—Eric Hoffer

Men are in trouble—everywhere in the world, at every level of society.

How are you supposed to be a man in today's world?

The messages are mixed, and the path is unclear. Cultural expectations keep shifting, and the old models no longer seem to fit.

Here's the common denominator: We were all boys once, and now we're men.

That's what matters.

This is about the journey every man makes—from the boy you were, to the man you've become, to the man who will need to reinvent and rediscover himself many times throughout the seasons of life.

What matters more than the things that make us different are the things that make us the same.

What we have in common is our shared humanity.

To illustrate a universal truth of our shared humanity, we need look no further than what it means to be a parent or grandparent. Think about it, every person, across all cultures and divides, deeply loves their children and fears for their safety and future.

While ancient conflicts and hatreds do exist, I believe the vast majority of beings everywhere yearn for a more peaceful world in which we can share and coexist.

Welcome to the honest, transparent, and rewarding work of transformational self-leadership. All that is required to be part of this movement is to be open to learning, growing, and evolving. I encourage you to embrace, as part of that, a willingness to support others and openly share what you learn.

The world needs people who are constant and never-ending learners.

In doing this work, you will meet many unexpected messengers and fellow travelers. Some will act as guides, several will serve as warnings and examples to avoid, and others will become your most trusted counsel.

Defining Transformational Self-Leadership

Transformational refers to the process of meaningful, deep personal change that moves you from conditioned patterns toward authentic self-expression. It's not about a sudden, dramatic overhaul but rather a gradual unfolding, where concentrated awareness in one area of life creates a "clarity cascade" that ripples outward, touching every other dimension of your being.

Transformation happens when you consciously engage with life's challenges and joys rather than merely reacting to them, allowing difficult experiences to become material for growth. It acknowledges that you examine the aspects of yourself shaped by upbringing, ego, and protective masks, so you can understand and integrate them in the service of becoming who you truly are beneath social conditioning. Transformation is not about achieving perfection but about intentional progress that naturally extends from your inner work into your relationships, work, and communities.

Self-leadership is the practice of consciously guiding yourself through life's journey rather than defaulting to external expectations or reactive patterns. It means taking ownership of your own growth and direction by developing across interconnected dimensions: knowing yourself, discovering meaning and purpose, clarifying values, practicing self-care, defining your roles and intentions, creating a vision, executing with consistency, cultivating willingness, and shaping your legacy.

Self-leadership operates from the inside out—beginning with authentic identity and conscious intention, then flowing into how you show up in your roles and the actions you take. It recognizes that before you can effectively lead others or contribute meaningfully to the world, you must first lead yourself with awareness, integrity, and purpose.

The Law of Reciprocity

Through the wisdom of our family matriarch, my great-aunt Glad, and from volunteering roughly 20 hours per week over the last 30+ years in support of men in transition and crisis, a clear-minded presence and commitment emerged that I refer to as The Law of Reciprocity.

When giving my time in support of others, I've learned the power and impact of:

1. Showing up, especially when most people don't
2. Doing what I say I'll do
3. "Give a shit" or don't help
4. Asking for nothing in return

So now, I ask you:

1. **Can you be relied upon to show up for others, especially when it counts?** If this isn't second nature already, through this work, it will be.
2. **Do you do what you say you will do?** If not, know that this doesn't define who you are. It represents an opportunity for growth.
3. **Do you genuinely care about the healthy outcomes of each person you choose to help?** If not, perhaps this is your inner wisdom helping you to discern where and with whom to invest yourself.
4. **Can you give of yourself and your gifts without expecting or needing something in return?** If at all possible, make a living from your work and profession so you can freely donate and invest your gifts and mentoring in the lives of others, especially younger generations.

These principles are foundational to *Men Harvesting Wisdom*. When you live by these principles, you find yourself sur-

INTRODUCTION: WHY THE TEN HEROIC DIMENSIONS EXIST

rounded by other men doing the same. We're everywhere—standing ready to lead, support, mentor, and be supported.

We need each other because this work—transformational self-leadership—isn't theoretical. It becomes urgent the moment life strips away the identity you've built.

You know the signs. Maybe you're living them right now. The guy who built his entire identity around his career gets forced into early retirement and has no idea who he is anymore. The father, whose kids have left home, realizes he doesn't recognize the man staring back at him in the mirror without a purpose. The husband whose wife left him because he wasn't really listening and "never did what you said you would." The Veteran who comes home from deployment and can't figure out how to be a husband, a father, and a civilian because while the uniform came off, the war never left.

Or maybe it's quieter than that. Maybe you're functional, successful even, but something's missing. You're going through the motions and working, providing, doing all the shit you're supposed to, but you can't shake the feeling that you're drifting instead of building something that matters. You're busy as hell, but you're not sure what any of it's for.

In my thirty years of working with at-risk Veterans, civilians from all walks of life, and their families, I've sat with countless men facing these moments. Here's what I've learned:

The crisis isn't what happened to you.

The crisis is that you don't know who you are without the thing that defined you.

That job you lost? That wasn't your identity, even though it felt like it was. That relationship that ended? That wasn't who you are, even though you organized your entire life around it. The vision that wasn't really yours, the role you excelled at that no longer exists, the legacy you lost?

You're still here. So who the hell are you now?

Too many guys try to outrun this question. They stay busy, start new projects, and throw themselves into whatever's next. Anything to avoid the silence where that question lives and persists: Who the hell am I now?

But you can't outrun it forever. The heroic journey for every man eventually calls, demanding that we engage in the relentless pursuit of becoming who we are meant to be. And when it does, you'll need a framework—not a theory or a trend, but something practical, tested in the real world by men who've been exactly where you are.

That's why this book—and this work—exists.

How I Know This Works

February 2004. My phone rang at midnight, which meant 3 a.m. in upstate New York. It was Danny, my son, calling from a snow-filled ditch behind his house.

In January, he'd returned home from his second deployment to Afghanistan. He'd spent nine years in the Army, some of them as a squad leader. He was a professional warfighter, respected by his men, galvanized into someone who knew exactly who he was and what he was capable of.

But for the first time in nearly a decade, without his uniform and stripped of his identity, Danny was lost and secretly terrified.

He'd put everyone to bed, locked the house, then positioned himself in a freezing, snowy ditch at the edge of his property, guarding his family from threats that existed only in his hypervigilant mind. He was chain-smoking cigarettes and joints, self-medicating with alcohol, and trying to quiet a nervous system that wouldn't stop scanning for danger.

INTRODUCTION: WHY THE TEN HEROIC DIMENSIONS EXIST

The myriad of mind-numbing prescription drugs weren't helping either.

"I don't know who I am without the uniform," he said, his voice barely above a whisper. And before he hung up, "I love you, Dad."

That was the beginning of months of late-night phone calls, and they always ended the same: I love you, Dad. Those four words became my own lifeline, proof that somewhere inside this tormented, self-medicating stranger, my son still existed. Danny was facing a complete identity collapse. Everything that had defined him—his rank, his mission, his purpose, his men—was gone. In its place was a void he didn't know how to fill.

During those conversations, patterns emerged. Three questions kept surfacing:

1. *Who am I now?*
2. *What do I do with my life?*
3. *I miss my men, my brothers.*

But these patterns weren't unique to just Danny.

Today, after three decades of working with at-risk Veterans and men in crisis, I can confirm these same three basic dilemmas exist for each and every man whose primary identity has been torn away. The specific circumstances change—it could be military transition, divorce, career loss, kids leaving home, death of a loved one, forced retirement—but the fundamental crisis remains the same.

Through those conversations, Danny and I broke down the overwhelming idea of "starting over" into four dimensions every man needs to rebuild his life: identity, mission, meaning, and purpose.

It worked. Danny got clear on who he wanted to become: a counselor for Veterans to help them through their transition from the military.

Once he had this new sense of clarity, I simply got out of the way. Danny gathered all of the necessary documentation, enrolled in a local community college, and graduated with his associate's degree. I helped him write a letter to Syracuse University, and he was accepted to earn a degree as a social worker.

Adjusting back into family life had its ups and downs, but he seemed to be self-medicating less.

All things considered, he was doing well. He was doing the work, but his time was cut short.

Even so, the simplicity of identity, mission, meaning, and purpose gave him back the mental and emotional compass he had misplaced when he separated from the service. Defining them with clarity gave him his grit back to move toward who he was becoming. All he really needed was a worthy objective.

Isn't that what we all need?

My own words echoed in my mind that I had shared with lost Veterans for years: identity, mission, meaning, purpose. I needed to look no further than my foundational work to find my compass, the one I'd misplaced at his funeral.

Since then, I've worked with all kinds of men—Veterans and civilians from all backgrounds—facing their own identity crises. A guy would gain clarity about his identity and purpose, but couldn't maintain the self-care necessary to sustain the journey. Another would have a compelling vision but lack the execution skills to make it real. Still others had everything mapped out but discovered they lacked the willingness to do what their own plans required.

INTRODUCTION: WHY THE TEN HEROIC DIMENSIONS EXIST

Each limitation revealed another dimension, another gap, another essential element that had to be addressed if the transformation was going to stick.

Eventually, I realized there aren't four dimensions.

There are ten.

These aren't abstract concepts developed in a classroom. Every dimension in this book has been tested in the most challenging circumstances imaginable: Veterans with PTSD, executives facing forced retirement, fathers whose marriages ended, men whose entire identity got ripped away, and who had to rebuild from the ground up.

That's what you're holding (or listening to), not just a book, but the culmination of years of pain, practice, and perseverance. What began as a desperate attempt to help one struggling Veteran has evolved into a reliable framework for helping people navigate change.

The Pattern Every Man Faces

Before we dive into the ten dimensions, you need to understand why they're heroic.

It's not because you're going to save the world or get a medal. It's because every meaningful transformation follows a pattern—one that numerous cultures have recognized throughout history. In fact, Joseph Campbell spent his life studying stories from civilizations around the world and discovered that the same basic storyline kept showing up.

He called it the Hero's Journey, and it goes like this:

You're living your ordinary life when something disrupts it, like a crisis, a loss, or something big that makes you realize you can't keep going the way you've been going. Maybe it's rock bottom. Maybe it's when you get what you thought you wanted, yet you feel empty inside. That's the call to adventure, whether you're ready or not.

At first, you resist. You try to stay comfortable to avoid the difficulty of change, but eventually, you cross a threshold. You commit to the journey of transformation.

Then come the trials. You face challenges that test you and force you to develop new capacities, revealing who you actually are beneath the persona you've been maintaining. You meet allies. You confront enemies, both external and internal. You descend into your own personal hell—"the belly of the whale," Campbell called it—where you either transform or get destroyed.

After you survive the ordeal, you gain something valuable, such as wisdom, clarity, and new capabilities. Then comes the hardest part: returning to your ordinary world as a changed man, bringing what you've learned back to serve others.

That's the arc from departure to return.

The Ten Heroic Dimensions you're about to explore are a map for finding your way back to yourself. They outline the essential elements every man needs to move through transformation with purpose and integrity. This isn't mythology; it's a lived pattern that echoes the journey of heroes across time. The difference is that this map is grounded in real life and in the struggle to rebuild when everything familiar has been lost. Whether you chose the change or it came crashing into you, these dimensions will help you remember who you are, rebuild what was lost, and become the healthiest version of who you're meant to be.

You're already on this journey, whether you realize it or not. The question is whether you're going to lead yourself through it consciously or just react to whatever comes at you.

These dimensions give you a way to lead.

What the Ten Heroic Dimensions Are:

Each one is essential, and each one synergizes with and builds upon the others.

The First Heroic Dimension: Identity: A foundational understanding of who you are. This is not who you've been performing as, but who you actually are beneath all the conditioning and adaptation. This is where transformation begins, because you can't build a meaningful life on a false version of yourself. Everything that follows depends on this.

The Second Heroic Dimension: Values: Fundamental principles and ideals that guide your choices and shape your future. Your values are your compass. When they're clear, decisions become simpler. When they're unclear or borrowed from someone else, you end up drifting.

The Third Heroic Dimension: Meaning: A personal sense that your life matters and that you have something of significance to contribute. Meaning is what makes suffering bearable (and like it or not, there is suffering in life, much of it unavoidable). It's what transforms pain into purpose. Without it, you're not living, you're just surviving.

The Fourth Heroic Dimension: Purpose: Direction, organization, and a plan of execution for actualizing what gives meaning to your life. Meaning is the "why." Purpose is the "how." It's the bridge between understanding what matters and actually doing something about it.

The Fifth Heroic Dimension: Self-Care: How you maintain and improve your physical, emotional, spiritual, and financial well-being. Most want to skip this chapter because they're literally scared of the word itself, but the fact is, you can't lead yourself effectively if you're broken down. Self-care is maintenance, and it isn't optional—it makes everything else sustainable.

The Sixth Heroic Dimension: Roles: The way you move through the world and how you intentionally show up. You

INTRODUCTION: WHY THE TEN HEROIC DIMENSIONS EXIST

play different roles throughout your day, but when those roles fragment your identity rather than express it, you end up exhausted and disconnected from yourself.

The Seventh Heroic Dimension: Vision: The compelling picture of your future that organizes your choices and drives your actions. Vision is what separates men who are drifting from men who are building something that matters. It's the future you create that's worth the struggle of getting there.

The Eighth Heroic Dimension: Execution: Moving from knowing what to do to actually doing it. A lot of guys get stuck here. They've got clarity, they understand the concepts, but they can't translate vision into a consistent plan of action. Execution is the dimension that makes everything else real.

The Ninth Heroic Dimension: Willingness: The choice to act when everything in you says not to. Willingness isn't about being willing when you already feel like it—that's momentum. Real willingness shows up when you don't want to do the thing, but you do it anyway because it aligns with who you said you'd be.

The Tenth Heroic Dimension: Legacy: The imprint and map you leave behind to help future generations navigate the world. Legacy isn't something you create at the end of your life. It's being built right now through your daily choices. When you start thinking about what will outlive you, you stop wasting time on shit that doesn't matter.

These dimensions work together.

Identity provides the foundation. Values guide the choices. Meaning gives the why. Purpose points the direction. Self-care maintains the capacity. Roles organize the expression. Vision creates the future. Execution makes it real. Willingness activates everything. Legacy integrates it all into something larger than yourself.

Staying Focused and Avoiding Overwhelm

I would like to suggest two approaches to using this work.

1. Take your time, go through all of the 10 dimensions one at a time.

2. Go to page 209 to learn about the process of triangulation to choose 1-3 relevant dimensions that need the most attention at this time.

Why Real Self-Leadership is Transformational

You become the leader of your own life by fundamentally changing how you think, behave, and motivate yourself from the inside out.

Men often treat themselves like projects to manage. They grind, they push, they force their way through resistance, running on willpower and borrowed motivation. It works for a while—until it doesn't. Eventually, it burns you out.

Real, transformational self-leadership is different. You inspire and influence yourself the same way a great leader would inspire their team. You create a vision that pulls you forward rather than having to push yourself constantly. You examine your values and beliefs instead of just accepting what you inherited. You develop intrinsic motivation and start doing things because they align with who you actually are, not just to avoid consequences or chase rewards.

And it's transformational because in doing this work, you will fundamentally reshape your identity, your mindset, and how you lead yourself through life.

So, for example, instead of "I need to exercise because I should lose weight," transformational self-leadership sounds like: "I value health and vitality. Movement, mobility, and fitness are part of living in alignment with who I am."

See the difference? You're not forcing behavior change from the outside. You're transforming your relationship with your mind and the behavior itself from the inside.

That's what these ten dimensions enable. They give you the mindset to lead yourself consciously instead of just reacting to whatever life throws at you.

How to Actually Use This

The goal isn't to read it once and move on—it's to live it.

The military uses a simple method to build mastery fast: Learn It. Teach It. Master It. You learn something important and pass it on, and through that cycle of learning and teaching, you internalize it.

That's the approach I'm borrowing here.

Learn It

After your initial read-through, don't take on all ten dimensions at once. That's a recipe for overwhelm and abandonment.

Either stop and obsess over whichever dimension captures your attention, or read through all of them to come back to the one that hurts the most.

Where are you feeling the most friction right now? A crisis of identity? Confusion about purpose? Neglecting your health? Roles pulling you in opposite directions? Start where the need is urgent, and your motivation is strongest.

Pick one dimension and go deep. Reread the chapter. Reflect on the questions. Do the work. Stay with it until you understand what's in your way, what needs attention, why it matters, and what specific steps you'll take next.

The power of this approach is that working deeply on one dimension naturally illuminates the others. When you gain clarity about your values, it affects how you understand your purpose. When you develop better self-care practices, your execution capacity improves. Nothing exists in isolation.

Teach It

As you begin to define these areas of your life, share what you're learning with someone. If you're refining your values or working on your vision, share that with a close friend. An accountability partner. A group of men in person or online. Your kids or the young adults in your life who could benefit from getting ahead of the learning curve.

Teaching forces clarity. When you have to explain something to another person, you discover whether you truly understand it or just think you do. More importantly, teaching creates accountability. When others know what you're working on and who you said you'd be, you're more likely to follow through.

I've found that when I put myself out there—doing what I told people I would do, being the man I said I would be—I feel better about myself, and I get shit done.

But there's an even deeper reason to teach these dimensions. Helping others transform reinforces your own transformation. Every time you guide someone through clarifying their values or defining their purpose, you strengthen those capacities within yourself.

Master It

Mastery isn't about perfect execution. It's about consistent application over time. It's about returning to these dimensions again and again, each time with deeper understanding and greater skill.

True mastery means these dimensions become part of your natural way of thinking. You don't have to consciously remember to consider your values when making decisions because it becomes automatic. You don't have to force yourself to think about your legacy because it naturally informs your choices.

That doesn't happen overnight. It happens through the cycle of learning, teaching, and living these dimensions until they're in your bones.

> **IMPORTANT PERSONAL USE NOTICE TO READER:**
>
> The Learn It, Teach It, Master It framework to master the Ten Heroic Dimensions presented here is designed for your personal growth and for sharing informally the concepts and ideas presented to friends, family, accountability partners, and fellow travelers on their own path of transformation.
>
> However, the content, frameworks, and methodologies in this book are protected intellectual property. They may not be used as the basis for commercial programs, workshops, coaching practices, consulting services, or any other for-profit endeavor without express written permission from the author.

The Mantra

I strongly suggest that you commit to memory the following mantra:

Progress, not perfection.

Don't focus on being perfect. Focus on being better than you were yesterday.

Remember, even monkeys fall from trees. If you find yourself falling back into what is familiar and comfortable, don't beat yourself up for too long. When we fall short of who we said we would be and what we said we would do, our failures and shortcomings act as constant reminders of why these ideals are important to us. Recognize when you are becoming triggered and beating yourself up. Realize that you can pause and convert regret, disappointment, or shame into fuel to ricochet yourself out of the cave where you tend to dwell on the past.

INTRODUCTION: WHY THE TEN HEROIC DIMENSIONS EXIST

The Work at the End of Each Chapter

At the end of every dimension, you'll find a section called "The Work."

I told you, this book isn't about theory or philosophy.

Reading about identity is one thing. Examining your own identity, taking a good look at the masks you wear, and writing about the parts that protect you and the conditioning that shaped you—that's where change happens. Similarly, reading about vision is interesting, but creating your specific vision and writing it down so you can return to it when things get hard is how you avoid being all talk and no action.

So, here's the deal. Get yourself a journal. A physical notebook, app on your phone, whatever works for you, but have it ready and use it.

Throughout this book, "The Work" sections will give you specific prompts and questions. Answer them. Write until you've captured what's true, even if it's uncomfortable (especially if it's uncomfortable). Record whatever comes up—single words, lists, brief statements, full paragraphs. The format doesn't matter. What matters is transferring thoughts from your mind onto a place where you can actually see them.

This is how you break the cycle of rumination. This is how patterns become visible. This is where you stop wrestling internally and start dealing with reality.

As you write, look for themes. The more you consider your words, the more will pour out. You might be starting this journey from relative peace—good upbringing, few major traumas, generally healthy disposition—or you might have spent years wrestling with internal conflicts and patterns you can't seem to break. Either way, this is your moment to face what's actually going on beneath the surface.

You are the sum of all your experiences and all the experiences you've avoided. The journal, the work, is where you examine both.

A Few Practical Guidelines

Realize that you'll return to these dimensions throughout your life. The identity work you do at thirty looks different from the identity work you do at fifty. The vision you create as a young father differs from the vision you hold as a grandfather. When you get married, your roles shift. When you change careers, your vision might need updating. When you face a health crisis, your self-care requires deeper examination. When you lose someone you love, your understanding of meaning and legacy transforms.

All that's normal. This framework isn't a one-time fix because you're not the same guy you were ten years ago, and you'll be a different guy ten years from now, too. This framework grows with you.

Remember, focus on progress, not perfection. You're going to make mistakes. You're going to have setbacks. You're going to discover gaps in your understanding. That's not failure—that's the learning process. Keep moving. Keep adjusting. Keep showing up for yourself.

Time to Begin

This work is hard. I'm not going to sugarcoat that.

It will ask you to examine things about yourself you've been avoiding. It demands that you face uncomfortable truths about who you've been and who you're becoming. It asks you to change patterns you've been reinforcing for decades. It will test your willingness to do what you said you'd do when everything in you wants to stay comfortable.

But here's what becomes possible when you do this work:

INTRODUCTION: WHY THE TEN HEROIC DIMENSIONS EXIST

You stop surviving by the skin of your teeth and start building something meaningful. You gain clarity about who you are and what you're here to contribute. You make decisions aligned with your actual values instead of borrowed expectations. You create a vision compelling enough to organize your daily choices around. You develop the capacity to execute consistently instead of just talking about change. You become someone who keeps commitments to himself and the people in his orbit. You leave behind something that matters.

It unleashes the most heroic version of yourself and lets you be that guy—forever.

Now, this framework can't do the work for you, but it can give you the structure, language, and navigation tools to lead yourself through transformation.

When you're lost—and you will get lost—you can use multiple dimensions simultaneously to figure out where you are and plot your course forward. Just like a hiker uses landmarks to pinpoint location, you can examine your values, assess your self-care, review your roles, and suddenly you're not completely adrift. You're at a specific intersection of circumstances that can be mapped and navigated.

So, here's the crucial question that precedes all navigation: Who is navigating?

Who are you?

Before you can plot a course toward who you're becoming, you need to understand who you are right now. Not who others think you are, not who you think you should be, not who you were before your last crisis, but who you actually are beneath all the bullshit and expectations and protective facades.

This is why we start with identity. It's the foundation upon which everything else rests.

Turn the page. Let's do the work.

THE FIRST HEROIC DIMENSION:

IDENTITY
A Foundational Understanding of Who You Are

"A man is not hurt so much by what happens as by his opinion of what happens. And our opinion of what happens is entirely up to us."

—Michel de Montaigne

Have you ever noticed yourself acting one way with your boss, another way with your significant other, your kids, and a completely different way with your oldest and closest friends?

These are examples of our conditioned ways of being, the alter egos and masks we wear to adapt and move through our daily interactions. Our adaptive nature is an essential part of being human.

Even when we're babies, we mold ourselves to deal with what we fear and to get what we need. We cry to be fed, to receive physical touch, and to have our diaper changed. These survival mechanisms mature with us, becoming more subtle and less obvious as we grow into adulthood. We all do it. It's our attempt to manipulate the world around us to create safety and comfort.

The more we learn to understand who we are and how we're showing up in the world, the easier it becomes to spot when we're being our real, authentic selves versus when we're shifting our communication and presence to serve a purpose. Sometimes these temporary personas are healthy and serve our greater good. But other personas can feel incongruent and fake.

There's a difference between being incongruent and inauthentic.

When I went through Army Airborne School during my time in the Marines, I looked the part: gear on, chin up, trying to project the kind of calm confidence the guys around me expected. On the outside, I was solid.

Inside, my emotions were swinging between panic and anticipation. My heart was pounding so hard I could feel it in my throat. My mouth was dry, my legs were restless, and I kept telling myself I was fine. I was cracking jokes, pretending it was just another day, but every cell in my body knew it wasn't.

I was incongruent. I looked ready and brave on the outside, but nothing was aligned internally. I mean, hell, I was about to jump out of a perfectly good airplane.

Inauthentic is different. Years later, I worked for a sales manager who was a poster child for inauthenticity. He had his routine down to an art. He'd kneel beside my desk, lay a hand on my shoulder, flash a practiced smile, and compliment my shoes, my tie, or my suit before asking for something. His words were smooth, and his timing was perfect, but something in my gut always clenched a half-second before he spoke.

You could feel the performance. It wasn't about connection; it was choreography. Every gesture had a purpose, and nothing was genuine.

He was inauthentic. Contrived. Manipulative.

Incongruence is the tension between what's real inside you and what you show the world. It feels uneasy, like holding your breath too long. If we are incongruent, it's often awkward and uncomfortable, which means we are out of our comfort zone and growing. So, instead of avoiding discomfort, try embracing it. Do this enough, and you will begin to feel a pull instead of a push against resistance.

Inauthenticity is being deliberately false. It feels hollow, like saying words that don't belong to you.

Knowing the difference and understanding which one you're dealing with in yourself and in others changes how you address it.

How We Got Here: The Conditioned Self

Your conditioned self is an integral part of who you are that learned how to survive before you learned to choose, and before you even knew you were being shaped.

We all came into the world as clean hard drives, and then life happened to us. All of your life experiences, and the parts of you they shaped, make up your conditioned self, building your tastes and preferences about the world around you.

Our conditioned self gets installed early through what our parents and families modeled for us, not just what they said. We absorbed their fears, their tempers, their avoidance, their addictions, their unspoken rules about love, money, success, and pain. Our culture and community layered on their own expectations of who we were supposed to be. But the strongest conditioning came from the emotional moments that cut the deepest—the times we felt unseen, unsafe, or unworthy—and the split-second decisions we made about who we had to be to survive them.

Our conditioned self is basically a puppet master; it's the part of you that's desperately attempting to manage your thoughts, impulses, and interactions. It has automatic triggers and responses, both good and bad.

Our conditioned self shows up in our automatic reactions, like when someone says something and before we can even think, we've already responded. This is conditioning at work, and it doesn't just control our reactions in the moment. It dictates who and what we're drawn to. The truth is, we're all walking around with these invisible "magnets" that pull us toward certain people and situations while pushing us away from others—for better or for worse, that's all based on patterns from our past.

Here's what you need to understand: Your conditioning isn't your fault, but it is your responsibility. You didn't choose what happened to you in childhood. You didn't choose your parents or your environment or the traumatic experiences that forced you to create survival strategies. But now, as an adult, you get to choose whether those old strategies still serve you or whether it's time to defragment and update your operating system.

The Parts That Protect You (And How to Work With Them)

You probably know what it's like to wrestle with the parts of yourself you wish you could get rid of. Maybe it's shame that won't quit, a need to always be right, or the way you shut down when criticized. Maybe it's perfectionism, people-pleasing, or that hair-trigger temper.

For decades, I attempted to kill off the parts of me I hated the most: my anger, my need for control, my sensitivity to being told what to do. But every attempt to kill these troubling parts only made them stronger. They became bigger to smack me down and remind me of the power they wield.

Then I learned about "Parts Work" from:

- **John Overdurf:** His work draws from Ericksonian hypnosis, Jungian depth psychology, neuroscience research, and contemplative traditions—synthesizing these into practical coaching applications that work below conscious mental processing to allow natural reframing and reconsolidation.

- **Richard Miller, PhD, creator of Integrative Restoration (iRest):** His approach helps people discover that seemingly opposing feelings or states are actually two sides of one coin, and that allowing both to be present leads to insight, integration, and wholeness. iRest has been extensively researched, particularly with Veterans for PTSD treatment, and was endorsed by the U.S. Army Surgeon General as a complementary medicine for chronic pain.

- **Dick Schwarz:** Creator of a parts framework called Internal Family Systems (IFS). IFS views every human being as a system of protective and wounded inner parts guided by a core Self. It teaches that the mind is naturally multiple—and that this multiplicity is healthy—because, like members of a family, inner parts can be pushed into extreme roles but also have valuable inherent qualities.

As I began to understand many of the internal conflicts I was carrying, my relationship with my conditioned self almost immediately changed. I realized these parts weren't enemies to destroy. They were protectors doing their best with the tools they developed when I was young and vulnerable.

Let me give you an example. In fifth grade, I was being bullied by a kid named Brian who outweighed me by thirty pounds. He grabbed my football, laughing while he shoved me to the ground. Every time I tried to get it back, he'd grab me by the face and fling me aside like a rag doll. I felt humiliated, small, powerless, and angry in a way I didn't have words for. Then suddenly, something welled up inside of me like Popeye downing a can of spinach. Without thinking, I jumped up and crushed his nose with a single blow of my fist. Blood rushed down his hands as he screamed, "You broke my nose!"

I stared at my fist, stunned. Where did that come from?

An enraged, protective part from deep within me had emerged and taken control. It took me five decades to understand that my capacity for violence is a part of me, but it isn't who I really am at the core. That part was created to protect the terrified kid who needed a defender. And once I understood that, things began to shift.

How to Identify Your Parts

Your parts show up in predictable patterns. You just have to start noticing them. Pay attention to:

- **The parts that take over when you're triggered.** What happens when someone criticizes you? Tells you what to do? Threatens your sense of control? Notice which part steps forward—the angry one, the defensive one, the one that shuts down completely.
- **The parts that protect you from pain.** Maybe you have a part that keeps you busy, so you don't have to feel. Or a

part that makes jokes when things get serious. Or a part that numbs out with substances, food, porn, work—anything to avoid vulnerable emotions.
- **The parts that carry old wounds.** These are the young, scared parts that still believe the world is as dangerous as it was when you were five or ten or fifteen. They're frozen in time, carrying fear and shame and beliefs about yourself that may not be true anymore.

Start noticing when these parts activate. You don't have to fix them or change them immediately. Just notice. "Oh, there's my controlling part. There's my defensive part. There's the part that thinks I'm not good enough."

How to Work With Your Parts

As I said, when I stopped trying to destroy my parts and started getting curious about them, everything changed.

When a part activates—when you feel that surge of anger or that need to control or that shame spiral starting—try this:

1. **Acknowledge it.** "I see you. I know you're here trying to have my back."
2. **Get curious.** "When did you first show up? What were you protecting me from? What do you need me to understand?"
3. **Thank it.** "Thank you for trying to keep me safe. I appreciate what you've been doing for me. I mean it."
4. **Reassure it.** "I'm an adult now. I have resources you didn't have when you were created. You can relax. You don't have to work so hard."

This isn't about getting rid of your parts. It's about updating their job descriptions. That angry part doesn't need to be on high alert 24/7 anymore. That controlling part doesn't need to micromanage every interaction. They can become advisors instead of dictators.

I found that if I approached my parts with curiosity instead of judgment, they would relax and tell me their stories. My shameful parts, my angry parts, my unlovable parts—each one was born out of necessity at a key moment in my life. Once they felt understood and appreciated for being my protectors, they began to take a seat as inner advisors rather than running the show.

The more I listened, the more peace I felt. The chaos inside quieted. Those parts stopped fighting for control because they finally trusted that the adult me was leading.

That's the real power of this work. When you start leading yourself with compassion and authority, you stop being at war with yourself. You become the steady center instead of the constantly shaping battlefield conditions in our mind.

Your Ego: The Reality Manager

Our ego isn't what most people think—it's not about being egotistical. Our ego is the essential part of us that helps us function in reality. It's like our personal assistant who helps us tell what's real from what's imagined, organizes our thoughts and plans our days, maintains our sense of "me" over time, and protects us from things that feel too overwhelming.

A healthy ego is flexible, handles uncertainty well, and can adapt to new situations without falling apart. But when our ego gets inflated, fragile, or too rigid—that's when we struggle.

You know your ego is out of balance when you can't handle feedback without falling apart, when you need constant validation to feel okay, or when you're so defensive that nothing gets through. A healthy ego can take a hit and recover. It can admit mistakes without your whole identity crumbling. It can be confident without being arrogant.

The work isn't to silence the ego. It's to lead it. A healthy ego keeps you grounded in reality and helps you show up as your full self. But when it starts overmanaging and trying to protect your image instead of your integrity, it creates something else entirely: the alter ego, a performer you send into the world when you don't feel safe being real.

After a hurt or devastating experience, the alter ego almost always comes out of the cave first to create a protective facade, mitigate threats, and forge the way forward.

The Alter Egos We Create

Ever notice how some people transform from their normal selves when they step onto a stage or into a boardroom? That's an alter ego at work, an alternative version of ourselves that we create to express dimensions that don't normally get to come out.

Mike Tyson's "Iron Mike" is a perfect example. Tyson has spoken about this alter ego as a separate entity, something he both depends upon and fears. "I'm always careful when that guy comes out," he said. "That guy haunts me. I wish that guy died, but he's here again." That's parts psychology in action. "Iron Mike" developed as a protective mechanism for the brutal world of boxing, but also created internal conflict.

I once bumped into one of my favorite UFC fighters, Cody Garbrandt, at a coffee shop in Vegas. His easygoing demeanor and the gentle handshake he offered shocked the hell out of me. In that moment, he was nothing like the fierce gladiator and showman I'd watched in the octagon. Since then, I've often wondered what alter ego he conjures up to become such a dominant competitor. If you want to see what I mean, check out his fight IQ with Dominic Cruz—wow!

The beautiful thing about alter egos is that they let us try on new ways of being without completely abandoning who we are. They're bridges to qualities we wish we had more of. The key is knowing when you're wearing the alter ego consciously versus when it has taken over without your awareness.

The Masks We Wear

We all wear masks. They're temporary personas we put on for different situations, like the Professional Mask for work, the Social Harmony Mask for family gatherings, and the Protective Mask when we feel vulnerable.

These masks help us navigate the different worlds we move through in a day. They're not about being deliberately false so much as they're about adapting appropriately to different contexts. But when we wear masks that deeply contradict our authentic feelings for too long, we become exhausted, disconnected from ourselves, and confused about who we really are.

We all wear masks—that's not in question. The question is: Are you wearing your masks consciously? Can you take them off when you're home? Or have you worn certain masks for so long that you've forgotten there's a face underneath? Because the danger isn't in wearing a mask—it's in mistaking it for your true identity. When that happens, you start performing instead of living, protecting a false identity instead of expressing your truth.

When you remember who you are underneath each mask, you gain the power to choose when, where, and why you put one on.

Pulling Back the Curtain

Until my early twenties, when I was introduced to personal development, I was too busy dealing with chaos to examine my own thought patterns. But one thing I often wondered was how my life would turn out.

So, have you ever wondered how your life would turn out?

Take a look at this moment.

Right now.

This is how your life turned out.

My own curtain-pulling moment came during a personal development workshop in my early thirties. The facilitator asked us to write a letter from our "higher self" to our "conditioned self." As I began writing, words poured out of me that I hadn't consciously formulated:

Dear John, I've been watching you run in circles for decades now, trying to prove your worth to people who can never be satisfied. You're giving too much, and your need for acceptance is out of balance. I'm your higher self, and I'm here whenever you're ready to put down that burden.

I sat, stunned, staring at the words. Where the hell did that come from? It didn't feel like something I'd written—it felt like something that had been waiting to be said. And as I read it again, the truth hit me: I'd been living other people's definitions of success, not my own.

Most people don't think about what they think about. Think about that.

They wake up and run the same mental programs, repeat the same stories, and react the same way to the same triggers, day after day, year after year.

This is your signal to stop and pay attention. Notice the voice in your head. Question the stories it tells you about who you are and what's possible.

What Happened to You: The ACEs Connection

In 2023, I listened to *What Happened to You?* by Oprah Winfrey and Dr. Bruce Perry on a long drive from Vegas to Santa Barbara and discovered the Adverse Childhood Experiences (ACEs) questionnaire—ten yes-or-no questions about childhood trauma. The higher your score, the more it predicts health problems later in life: heart disease, diabetes, hypertension, depression, substance abuse, and even early death.

I scored nine out of ten. Pretty devastating for a guy in his sixties.

I kept listening, and I'm glad I did. For my entire life, I'd felt the only way to interpret my suffering was that something had to be wrong with me.

But Oprah shared a realization that hit me like a bolt of lightning: Nothing was wrong with her. Bad things had happened to her.

Reframing "What's wrong with me?" to "What happened to me?" is incredibly powerful. As I sat there letting this insight sink in, I realized how long I'd been carrying the wrong conclusion about something being wrong with me and how heavy it had become.

The burden of shame I'd carried for six decades began to lift. It didn't happen all at once. It was more like something unclenching deep in my chest, a tension I'd normalized and hadn't even realized I'd been holding. For the first time, I wasn't trying to fix or outrun the pain; I was simply witnessing it.

The tired kid within me—the one who'd been hustling for approval and bracing for rejection his entire life—finally exhaled. He felt seen. He felt understood. And in that quiet recognition, I felt something I hadn't felt in years: peace.

Why This Matters for You

The ACEs questionnaire isn't about labeling yourself as damaged. It's about understanding why you developed the protective patterns you did.

If you score high on the ACEs, it explains why your nervous system is wired for hypervigilance, why you struggle with trust, and why you developed those protective parts we talked about earlier. It's not a life sentence—it's information.

Importantly, ACEs scores predict negative health outcomes for people who don't do the work. But if you're reading this book, you're already doing the work. Every therapeutic intervention, every personal development retreat, every honest conversation, every moment of self-awareness—it all counts. You're not powerless. You're reclaiming years, maybe decades, of your life.

As stated on the very first page of this book, here's a mantra I've learned to live by: "No matter what I have been through, no matter how traumatic or heartbreaking, I deserve to live a fulfilling life."

Let that settle in. You may not feel it's true yet. You may have normalized struggling and suffering. But I've discovered that's an untruth. After decades of suffering, I found an off-ramp. There is a way forward. If you don't like something about your life as it is right now, you have the power to change it.

And as I began to live a more fulfilling life, the next mantra somehow finally felt okay too: "I deserve to be happy."

Healing is about reclaiming your relationship with the past. Your history doesn't define you; it informs you. Every insight and every small act of awareness is a step toward freedom. And when you begin to see your story through that lens, you realize something extraordinary: You were never broken. You were adapting. And now, you're evolving.

Your Work: Getting to Know Yourself

So, how do you actually start this work of understanding your identity, your conditioning, and your parts?

- **Start tracking your patterns.** For the next week, pay attention to your automatic reactions. When do you get triggered? What situations activate which parts? Just notice. Don't judge. Write it down.
- **Identify your top three protective parts.** Maybe it's the angry one, the controlling one, the people-pleasing one, the one that needs to be liked, the one that needs to be included. Name them. Get curious about when they first showed up. What were they protecting you from?
- **Ask yourself about the masks you're wearing.** Which ones serve you? Which ones are exhausting you? Where are you performing, rather than being yourself?
- **Consider taking the ACEs questionnaire.** I can't recommend this one enough. I've added it to "The Work" section at the end of this chapter, but you can also find it online. Whatever your score, remember that it's information, not destiny. It explains your wiring. It doesn't define your future.
- **Look for your curtain-pulling moments.** Are you living someone else's definition of success? When are you running on autopilot, repeating patterns that no longer serve you?

Self-awareness gives us a better understanding of the relationship between our thoughts, feelings, and actions. The more you understand why you do what you do, the more compassion you develop for yourself and the more power you have to choose differently.

Getting to know yourself is a crucial part of self-leadership. It's how you stop being driven by your past and start creating your future—one conscious moment at a time.

The Journey Toward Wholeness

Remember that the journey to being your best self isn't centered around getting rid of any of these parts. It's centered around bringing them into harmony.

When you become more aware of all these aspects of yourself, you gain the power to choose. You can consciously decide which conditioned patterns to keep and which to release. You can strengthen your ego in healthy ways. You can create alter egos that help you grow. You can wear masks mindfully, staying connected to your authentic self underneath.

The goal isn't to be mask-free, conditioning-free, or even ego-free. The goal is to be aware, to be intentional, and to align all these parts of yourself with who you're actually meant to be—not who your father said you should be, not who your culture expects, not the sanitized version that gets approval. The real you underneath all the conditioning and protection and adaptation.

Wholeness isn't about perfection—it's about integration. It's when the noise in your head settles, the fight inside you eases, and you start leading your life from truth instead of survival. That's real freedom, and it starts right now, with one steady breath and one honest decision at a time.

INNER WORK SECTION

NOTES

THE WORK (Grab your journal!)

Who are the different versions of you that show up when you need them most?

1. **Identify your alter egos.** When do you become someone different? Maybe it's when you step into a big meeting, when you're coaching your kid's team, when you're negotiating a deal, or when you need to handle conflict. Give each alter ego a name—it doesn't have to be dramatic, just something that captures the essence of that version of you.

2. **For each one, describe:** What does this alter ego give you access to? What qualities, capabilities, or behaviors emerge that don't normally show up in your everyday life? Is it confidence? Aggression? Playfulness? Authority? Fearlessness?

3. **Get curious.** Which of these alter egos serves you well? Which one might be running the show too often or showing up in situations where it doesn't belong?

4. **Think about one alter ego you wish you could access more intentionally.** What would it look like to consciously summon this version of yourself when you need it most? What would need to happen for you to give yourself permission to step into that role?

Write it down.

Now, keep in mind that wholeness isn't just about who you are today. It's also about where the hell you came from. Your habits, your triggers, your protectors, your armor—none of that was formed in a vacuum. Most of it was built when you were young, doing whatever you had to do to survive in your environment.

So, now it's time to take an honest, grounded look at the experiences that shaped you. Not to blame anybody or to get stuck in the past, but to understand the architecture of your inner world.

Take the ACEs Questionnaire

Instructions: Below is a list of 10 categories of Adverse Childhood Experiences (ACEs). From the list below, please place a checkmark next to each ACE category that you experienced prior to your 18th birthday. Then, please add up the number of categories of ACEs you experienced and put the *total number* at the bottom.

1. Did you feel that you didn't have enough to eat, had to wear dirty clothes, or had no one to protect or take care of you?	☐
2. Did you lose a parent through divorce, abandonment, death, or other reason?	☐
3. Did you live with anyone who was depressed, mentally ill, or attempted suicide?	☐
4. Did you live with anyone who had a problem with drinking or using drugs, including prescription drugs?	☐
5. Did your parents or adults in your home ever hit, punch, beat, or threaten to harm each other?	☐
6. Did you live with anyone who went to jail or prison?	☐
7. Did a parent or adult in your home ever swear at you, insult you, or put you down?	☐
8. Did a parent or adult in your home ever hit, beat, kick, or physically hurt you in any way?	☐
9. Did you feel that no one in your family loved you or thought you were special?	☐
10. Did you experience unwanted sexual contact (such as fondling or oral/anal/vaginal intercourse/penetration)?	☐
Your ACE score is the total number of checked responses	

Do you believe that these experiences have affected your health?   ○ Not Much   ○ Some   ○ A Lot

THE SECOND HEROIC DIMENSION:

VALUES

Fundamental principles and ideals that guide your choices and shape your future

"Your beliefs become your thoughts. Your thoughts become your words. Your words become your actions. Your actions become your habits. Your habits become your values. Your values become your destiny."

— Mahatma Gandhi

I spent the second half of my twenties making decisions that looked good on paper but felt toxic in my gut. Took a string of jobs with some prestigious companies because that's what success was supposed to look like. Said "yes" to obligations that drained me because I thought I had to prove myself and didn't want to disappoint people.

Every single one of those decisions made sense at the time.

And every single one of them moved me further away from who I actually was.

I began to see myself as chronically dissatisfied in every aspect of my life.

Can you relate to this on any level?

Maybe you've done everything "right"—worked hard, stayed loyal, hit the marks—and still feel that low-grade chronic dissatisfaction you can't explain. You've got the job, the relationship, the house, the checklist, but something in your gut knows this can't be all there is.

What I didn't understand then was that I was living by values I'd absorbed from everyone else—parents, friends, work associates, even cultural influences like movies and TV—instead of values I'd actually chosen for myself. And until I got clear on what genuinely mattered to me, not what I thought should matter, I kept making choices that left me feeling disconnected from my own life.

If you've ever found yourself conflicted about a major life decision (or even just a Tuesday afternoon when nothing feels quite right), chances are you're working against what you actually value. Most of us have to make a lot of poor decisions before we realize we even have values, let alone how to use them.

Your Internal Compass

Think of your values like a compass, the kind you need to read when you're in unfamiliar territory and the trail markers have disappeared.

During Naval Gunfire school on a remote island of the Philippines, we were put through a grueling jungle training and night compass course. As a team, we navigated through the swampy and razor-sharp jagged rocks. The compass didn't tell us exactly where to go, it just showed us which direction we needed to head toward. The rest was up to us—reading terrain, making judgment calls, and adjusting course when we hit an obstacle. But without that consistent reference point? We'd have been walking in circles.

Your values work the same way. They don't give you a detailed map of your life or tell you exactly what to do in every situation. What they do is give you a reference point. When you're facing a decision—whether it's a career change, an interpersonal relationship question, or how you're spending your time—you can orient yourself by asking, "Which direction moves me closer to what I actually value?"

The compass is most valuable when you're in terrain you've never covered before: a new job offer in a different city, an opportunity that requires sacrifice, a relationship that challenges everything you thought you wanted. These are the moments when you need to know what your true north actually is.

And here's the thing about a compass: it doesn't lie to you based on what looks appealing. That lucrative job opportunity might seem like the obvious choice, but if it requires you to compromise on work-life balance and you've got young kids at home, your values compass is telling you something important. That's not the path. Or maybe it is, but you need to be honest about the trade-off you're making.

Remember, the compass can't walk the trail for you. It can only point you toward alignment. Self-leadership is in the discipline of checking it often, particularly when the way ahead looks uncertain or tempting. Guys get lost not because they don't have a compass, but because they stop looking at it. So, keep yours close, and keep a close eye on it. And when the noise of the world tries to pull you off course, trust the direction that feels steady, not the one that looks easy.

What Makes Something a Value

Values aren't the same as preferences or goals. I prefer dark roast coffee, and I have a goal to bench press 225 pounds. Those can change tomorrow, and I'm still fundamentally me.

But my values? Those are the deeper currents. They're what I come back to when everything else strips away. They shape how I show up as a husband, how I conduct business, what I'm willing to compromise on, and what I'm not.

Values are the principles you're willing to defend even when it costs you something.

Real values have some specific qualities:

1. **They're hierarchical.** Some matter more than others, and that hierarchy guides you when values conflict. You might value both ambition and family time, but when your kid's soccer game conflicts with a career opportunity, which one wins? That's your hierarchy showing itself.

2. **They transcend specific situations.** A value doesn't change based on whether it's convenient. If you value integrity, that applies whether you're negotiating a deal or explaining to your son why you can't make his game.

3. **They feel non-negotiable.** Not rigid—you'll grow, and your understanding will deepen—but there's a line. Cross it, and something in you says, "No, not that."

Keep in mind that your values aren't fully formed when you're twenty. Hell, they're not fully formed when you're forty. They develop through experience, through reflection, through the times you violate them and feel that gut-punch of being out of integrity with yourself.

You have values. Everyone does. But too many guys have never identified them clearly enough to use them. They're still operating on autopilot with values they inherited and never examined. The thing is, when your values are clear, your decisions become clear, especially when they're difficult.

Your values are the internal code you live by. They're the difference between reacting and responding, drifting and deciding, fitting in and standing firm. When you know what you stand for, life doesn't get easier, but it does get simpler. You stop chasing approval and start moving with purpose. That's what real clarity feels like.

The Universal Patterns (And Why They Matter)

I've noticed in my own life and in working with men over the years that certain patterns keep showing up.

Connection matters to us. Not the superficial networking bullshit, but real relationships where you can be yourself. The guys who deny this, who pride themselves on being lone wolves? They're usually the most isolated and miserable.

We want autonomy. The ability to make our own choices, to direct our own lives. I've watched capable men wither in environments where every decision gets micromanaged, where they have no real agency. It breaks something in us.

We care about fairness, even if we don't always admit it. When we see someone getting screwed over or notice the game is rigged, it pisses us off. Some of us organize our entire lives around fighting for justice. Others just want to know they're playing on a level field.

We seek security and safety. Yeah, we value that too, though we're often terrible at acknowledging it. We'll sacrifice sleep, health, relationships, all in pursuit of feeling secure. Sometimes that's necessary. Sometimes we're just scared.

And then there's truth and knowledge. Achievement and mastery. The desire to be competent at something, to meet challenges and not come up short. Care and compassion, even though that one makes some guys uncomfortable to name. The need for balance, for creativity, for leaving something behind that matters.

I'm not telling you these should be your values. I'm saying these patterns exist in human nature, and understanding them helps you identify what's actually driving you versus what you think should be driving you.

Once you start recognizing these universal patterns in yourself, you stop being run by them. You start working with them. You can build real connections without losing your edge. You can value safety without letting fear dictate your choices. You can pursue mastery without letting achievement define your worth.

This is what it means to be a healthy, grounded, self-led man—not rejecting these drives, but integrating them. When you understand what truly motivates you, you stop living reactively and start leading intentionally. That's the difference between drifting through life and owning your direction.

When Your Values Go to War With Each Other

This part gets messy. Your values don't always play nice with each other.

I remember the exact moment I realized my value of security was suffocating my value of freedom. I'd built this comfortable life: good income, predictable routine, minimal risk. It was safe, and I was fucking miserable because I'd engineered out every bit of autonomy and adventure that made me feel alive.

Or take the classic conflict every parent knows: achievement versus family time. You value being excellent at your work. You also value being present for your family. But the deal that could transform your business requires you to miss your daughter's birthday. Now what?

There's no clean answer. Anyone who tells you otherwise is selling something.

Some guys respond to these conflicts by going rigid, picking one dominant value and sacrificing everything else on that altar. I've seen men destroy their health in pursuit of achievement, blow up their marriages in pursuit of freedom, or compromise their sense of integrity in pursuit of security. The value they chose might be legitimate, but the cost is devastating.

The better approach—though it's harder—is learning to honor multiple values even when you can't fully satisfy all of them. Maybe you take the business deal, but you fly home for the birthday, even if it's expensive and exhausting. Maybe you turn down the deal and find a different path to growth. The point is you're conscious about the trade-off instead of pretending it doesn't exist.

What matters is that you're making the choice deliberately, with your eyes open, rather than letting circumstances decide for you.

How Values Change Whether You Want Them To Or Not

I used to value recognition more than I do now. In my twenties and early thirties, being seen as successful mattered enormously. I made decisions based on how they'd look to others and what they'd signal about my status.

That's shifted. Not because I decided it should, but because life beat it out of me through enough experiences where, in the end, external validation felt hollow compared to internal alignment.

Your values will evolve. Research shows this happens pretty consistently. We tend to move from self-focused concerns when we're younger toward more transcendent, legacy-oriented values as we mature. But it's not automatic, and it's not always comfortable.

The evolution usually happens through friction. You violate a value you didn't know you had and get that familiar sick feeling in your stomach. Or you achieve something you thought would matter and discover it doesn't. Or something breaks—a relationship, a job, your health—and suddenly your priorities reorganize themselves whether you like it or not.

The men I respect most aren't the ones whose values never changed. They're the ones who got honest about the change instead of clinging to outdated versions of themselves.

That's real self-leadership in my view—being willing to stand in the tension between competing values without losing yourself in the process. A healthy, grounded, self-led man doesn't chase balance; he practices alignment. He makes the hard calls, owns the trade-offs, and moves forward with clarity instead of guilt.

But I have to remind myself and forgive myself from time to time. As I mentioned in the intro, even monkeys fall from trees, and this is about progress, not perfection.

When I have ignored what I know to be true and good for me, like indulging in foods that are bad for me, I don't live there long. I acknowledge the choice and stop the cycle of shame from ramping up. And I've learned to indulge by savoring just a bite or two instead of plowing through the whole plate.

From Theory to Reality

Your values mean exactly nothing until they're lived.

THE SECOND HEROIC DIMENSION: VALUES

You can have the most beautifully articulated value system in the world. You can journal about it, talk about it with your therapist, and have it written on a card in your wallet. But if your daily choices don't reflect those values, you're just carrying around nice-sounding concepts.

Values become real when they cost you something. When you turn down the lucrative opportunity because it conflicts with your integrity. When you have a difficult conversation because you value honesty over comfort. When you rearrange your life because your current setup violates what you actually care about.

This is why defining your values matters—not as an intellectual exercise, but as the foundation for how you actually move through the world. As I said before, when your values are clear, decisions become simpler. Not easier—simpler. You know what you're optimizing for. You know what you're willing to sacrifice and what you're not.

I've watched this create remarkable clarity for men who were drowning in options and obligations. Once they got clear on their core values, they could look at their calendar, their commitments, their relationships, and ask: "Does this align with what I value, or am I just doing it because I always have?"

That question changes everything. It transforms life from reactive and responding to whoever's loudest or whatever seems most urgent to deliberate. You're not living by default anymore. You're living by design.

And when hard times come—and they will come—your values become an anchor. Research backs this up: people who can connect their suffering to deeply held values recover faster from trauma and demonstrate more resilience. It's not that the pain hurts less because, believe me, it hurts like hell. The difference is that it means something. You're enduring it for a reason that matters to you.

That's the whole point of this work: to live in a way that's congruent, not convenient. To act in alignment with who you say you are, not who the world pressures you to be. That's what separates a man who reacts from a man who leads—a man who can stand in his values even when it costs him something, because he knows what those values are worth.

Get Real and Get Used to It

Living your values isn't a one-time declaration. It's a daily practice of checking whether your life reflects what you say matters most.

This requires brutal honesty. You have to be willing to look at the gap between your stated values and your actual behavior. Maybe you say you value health, but you're forty pounds overweight and haven't exercised in six months. Maybe you say you value your marriage, but you've been emotionally checked out for years. Maybe you say you value integrity, but you're cutting corners in your business.

The gap doesn't make you a hypocrite. It makes you human. What makes you grow is acknowledging the gap and then deciding whether to close it—either by changing your behavior or by being honest that maybe that thing you thought you valued isn't actually a priority for you right now.

The men who live the most integrated lives aren't the ones who never fall out of alignment. They're the ones who notice quickly when they drift, and they course-correct before the drift becomes their new normal.

INNER WORK SECTION

NOTES

THE SECOND HEROIC DIMENSION: VALUES

THE WORK (Grab your journal!)

Think about the values that consistently guide your most meaningful decisions. When have you felt most aligned and authentic in your life, and what values were you honoring in those moments?

Conversely, when have you felt internal conflict? Which values are you not honoring that may explain the discomfort?

Find a quiet place where you can really think and fill out the following, reflecting honestly about what matters to you—not what sounds good in theory:

VALUES

Personal values are the fundamental principles and ideals that guide your choices, shape your character and define what matters most to you.

When we deepen our understanding of who we are, we expand the potential for who we are becoming and what we can accomplish.

"I know and understand my personal values."

Absolutely disagree 1 2 3 4 5 Absolutely Agree

"My personal values help guide important decisions in my life."

Absolutely disagree 1 2 3 4 5 Absolutely Agree

"I am living in integrity with my personal values and happy with my progress."

Absolutely disagree 1 2 3 4 5 Absolutely Agree

Personal Values Exercise

Step 1: Initial Review
Below is a list of 60 core values. Read through the entire list first to get familiar with all options.

THE 60 VALUES

○ Achievement	○ Faith	○ Integrity	○ Recognition
○ Adventure	○ Fame	○ Intelligence	○ Religion
○ Authenticity	○ Family	○ Justice	○ Reputation
○ Authority	○ Freedom	○ Knowledge	○ Responsibility
○ Balance	○ Friendship	○ Leadership	○ Security
○ Beauty	○ Fun	○ Learning	○ Self-Respect
○ Challenge	○ Growth	○ Legacy	○ Service
○ Community	○ Happiness	○ Leisure	○ Spirituality
○ Compassion	○ Health	○ Loyalty	○ Stability
○ Competence	○ Honesty	○ Money	○ Success
○ Courage	○ Hope	○ Nature	○ Tradition
○ Creativity	○ Humility	○ Order	○ Travel
○ Curiosity	○ Independence	○ Pleasure	○ Truth
○ Excellence	○ Influence	○ Popularity	○ Wealth
○ Excitement	○ Inner Harmony	○ Power	○ Wisdom

THE SECOND HEROIC DIMENSION: VALUES

Step 2: First Cut (15-20 values)

Go through the list and circle or write down any value that resonates with you—don't overthink it. This will provide 15-20 values that are important to you.

Step 3: The Sorting Process

Sort your 15-20 values into three piles:

Very Important (5-7 values)	Important (5-7 values)	Somewhat Important (remaining values)

Step 4: The Hard Choices

From your "Very Important" pile, you need to eliminate all but 5. For each potential elimination, ask yourself:

"If I had to choose between this value and my current top 5, which would I choose?"

"What would I regret more, not pursuing this value, or not pursuing the others?"

"What would I regret more, not pursuing this value, or not pursuing the others?"

Step 5: Define Your Values

Write 2-3 sentences describing what each of your top 5 values means to you personally. Generic definitions aren't enough - make them specific to your life and aspirations.

This exercise typically takes 30-45 minutes and works best when done in a quiet space where you can reflect honestly about what matters most to you.

THE THIRD HEROIC DIMENSION:

MEANING

A personal sense that your life matters and that you have something of significance to contribute

"*In times of crisis, people reach for meaning. Meaning is strength. Our survival may depend on our seeking and finding it.*"
—Viktor Frankl, Man's Search For Meaning

Have you ever had a moment where you looked at your life and thought, "Is this all there is?" Or, "What's the fucking point of any of this?"

As the great philosopher Jim Rohn would say, "These are called clues." Clues that you have lost your sense of what brings meaning to your life.

Meaning doesn't disappear all at once. It slips away in moments we don't always notice.

Maybe it happened after losing a loved one. Maybe during a transition—divorce, job loss, kids leaving home. Maybe it just crept up on you one Sunday morning when you were ruminating about dreading going back to work on Monday, and you suddenly realize you've been going through the motions for months, years, or even decades, and nothing feels like it matters.

That's an existential crisis, and I'm not going to sugarcoat it—it's brutal. Everything you thought gave your life meaning suddenly feels hollow. The goals you were chasing seem arbitrary. The routines that kept you moving feel empty. You're standing in the middle of your existential dilemma, asking, "Why am I doing any of this?" and you don't have a good answer.

And when that emptiness shows up, most of us don't know what to do with it.

It's not uncommon for guys to try to outrun this feeling. They get busier. They throw themselves into work, start a new project, pick up a hobby, maybe have an affair, or buy a motorcycle. Anything to fill the void without actually looking at it.

After I lost my son, I spent months in a numb, detached state where nothing felt meaningful or hopeful. I knew intellectually that I should care about things, but I couldn't access that feeling. Everything was gray. Food had no taste, mornings had no pull, and even the things I used to care about felt like they belonged to someone else.

I was in a deep state of depression, and I wasn't sure if I wanted to be here. That scared me straight back into this work, and here's what I learned: You can't fill an existential void with busyness or distraction. You have to go through it. You have to ask the hard questions, because on the other side of that despair is where you find what actually gives your life meaning.

THE THIRD HEROIC DIMENSION: MEANING

The Question Nobody Wants to Ask

Meaning is fuel, not a luxury.

When I meet with a man in crisis, I don't focus on fixing anything or throwing solutions at him. It's to get curious about what and who matters to him and why.

The existential why.

Not "Why did this happen to me?" but "Why does anything matter to me at all?" It's a question many people spend years avoiding, because once you face it, you can't hide behind your old life anymore.

This is uncomfortable territory. It's easier to stay on the surface, to self-medicate, to stay numb, to keep moving, to avoid the big questions. But if you're reading this chapter, you're probably already asking those questions. Something has disrupted your sense of meaning, and you can't unring that bell.

So, let's go there. Let's talk about what actually gives life meaning, how you find it, and why the search itself might be the most important work you ever do.

What Drives Us (And What Doesn't)

Sigmund Freud called it the "pleasure principle"—we move toward what feels good and away from what feels bad. Makes sense, right? Except it's not quite that simple.

Tony Robbins sharpened this into something more accurate: "People will do more to avoid pain than to gain pleasure." That's the real driver for most of us. We're not primarily motivated by chasing what we want. We're motivated by avoiding what we fear.

Think about your own choices. How many of them are driven by fear of consequences rather than genuine desire? You stay in the unfulfilling job because you're scared of financial instability. You avoid a hard conversation because you're afraid of conflict. You keep your head down because you don't want to risk failure or rejection.

Fear works. That's why fear-based marketing is so effective. That's why negative feedback hits us harder than positive feedback. That's why so many of us spend our lives in a defensive crouch, trying not to lose rather than actually trying to win.

The great philosopher Earl Nightingale wrote and recorded the following in 1956, and said it well:

"The most unrewarding game is not following the leader, but follow the follower. The question we must ask ourselves is: Are the people I'm following going where I want to go?"

If we keep marching, numb and hollow, we will never know.

The problem is that while fear and numbing out might keep you safe, they don't give you meaning. You can spend your entire life avoiding pain and never actually discover what matters to you. You survive, but you don't live.

The Call That Changed Everything

Let me tell you about the moment my understanding of meaning shifted from theory to lived experience.

November 3rd, 2003. 11 a.m. Pacific time. I was sitting on my couch, half-watching the news about the war in Afghanistan, when my phone rang.

"Hello?"

Danny's voice cracked through satellite phone static. "Dad, I'm calling from a satellite phone. I don't have much time. Can you hear me?"

I bolted upright. "Danny? Yes, I can hear you. Where are you?"

THE THIRD HEROIC DIMENSION: MEANING

"I can't say, but..." The silence stretched. "I'm just too fucked up to come home."

I pulled the phone away from my ear and looked at it in shock, trying to process what I'd just heard.

Danny continued, "I've just seen too much, done too much. We lost some guys. I don't remember what it's like to be a husband or a father. I'm just too fucked up to come home."

I can count my most traumatic experiences on all my fingers and toes, but as a parent, this moment haunts me the most.

I can't think of anything worse than being helpless when your child needs you. And in that moment, listening to my son's voice crack with pain from the other side of the world, I was completely helpless.

Danny was calling from one of the most dangerous forward operating bases in Afghanistan, just three miles from the Pakistan border, where his unit faced near-daily firefights. He'd lost several men in the violent exchanges, and the death of one in particular left him feeling crushed by survivor's guilt. He was exhausted and beaten down, wondering if he'd survive what the war had done to his mind.

All I could manage was, "Just get home alive, son. I'll have some things lined up to get you through this. Just get home alive."

His hollow response: "Got to go, Dad. I love you."

I sat numb for hours after that call, trying to process what had just happened.

When Danny finally made it home in early January 2004, emotionally, he was in pieces. His first morning back, he called me in a panic: "Just a few days ago, I was killing this fucker on the side of a mountain, and now I'm cooking eggs for my kid. What the hell! I can't get my head around this?"

Over the months that followed—through late-night conversations and the framework we built together that I mentioned in the introduction—Danny began finding his way. He discovered that his suffering could become his qualification, his trauma could become his credibility. He could turn his pain into service by helping other Veterans navigate what he was going through. By earning a degree in social work, he would be on the other side of the table, helping Veterans instead of the well-intentioned civilian counselors he was forced to see. They were incredibly qualified and effective, but because they hadn't walked in his boots, he couldn't hear them.

His plan worked—until his life was cut short.

Forging Meaning From the Void

I stumbled across Viktor Frankl's *Man's Search for Meaning* at Barnes & Noble. It practically jumped off the shelf at me. Reading about this man who survived Nazi concentration camps—who watched almost everyone he loved die and endured unimaginable horror—and still found meaning changed something in me.

Viktor Frankl was a psychiatrist and neurologist who brought his professional training into the concentration camps with him. He observed, even amid unimaginable suffering, how prisoners responded to their circumstances. While survival depended on countless factors often beyond anyone's control, Frankl noticed patterns in how people faced unthinkable brutality. Those observations became the foundation for work that has profoundly impacted countless people who are suffering. His insights will live on forever.

Frankl's core insight was that humans are primarily motivated by the search for meaning, especially when confronting seemingly meaningless suffering. The prisoners who maintained a sense of meaning—even in hell—had a stronger chance of survival. Not because meaning protected them from suffering, but because it gave them a reason to endure it.

That realization hit me hard. I was at a crossroads. I could retreat, turtle up, and let the grief destroy me, or I could embark on creating new meaning from this loss. Suddenly, with this clarity that felt both simple and profound, I knew what gave my life meaning: helping others who are suffering.

I became the Wounded Healer. As long as I moved my pain, it wouldn't eat me alive.

I didn't know how that would unfold exactly. I didn't have a plan, but I knew my aim was true. I was meant to make a difference in the lives of other men—especially Veterans coming home from war—as my path through this grief. That became my north star.

I kept thinking about those late-night conversations with Danny. I realized that even in death, Danny could still help bring warriors home alive. Not just physically alive, but emotionally alive. The work we'd started together didn't have to die with him.

That became my meaning: to honor his struggle by helping other men navigate their own crises of identity and purpose. To transform my grief into service. To prove that even the most devastating loss can be woven into something larger.

When Despair Cracks You Open

There's a painful paradox I've seen play out over and over: moments of deep despair are often the ones where we unexpectedly discover our most profound sources of meaning.

And let me be clear: I'm not romanticizing suffering. I'm not saying "everything happens for a reason." Loss is loss. Pain is pain. This isn't about positive thinking or pretending tragedy is a gift.

But there is something that happens when life cracks you open that nothing else can replicate. When the bottom drops out, all the superficial shit we've built our identities on falls away. The bravado, the armor, the titles, the goals you thought were worth everything. Suddenly, the things you were chasing look small. You lose your grip on the things you were clinging to. The noise dies down, and what's left is a brutal kind of clarity, the kind you don't get when life is going well.

In that emptiness—that exposed place where nothing feels solid—you come face-to-face with questions you've spent years avoiding:

What is my life actually for?

Who am I without the roles I play?

What still matters when everything else burns away?

If any of this hits uncomfortably close, you're not broken. You're waking up. Meaning doesn't come from suffering itself. Plenty of men get crushed by it. Meaning comes from what you do with that suffering—from whether you face what cracked you open or run from it.

Find What Really Resonates

How does this actually work? How does despair transform into meaning instead of destroying you?

It starts when you confront mortality—your own or someone else's.

When you're forced to see that life is finite, that time is limited, that death is real and can take someone you love without warning, everything superficial falls away. The petty shit. The status games. The goals you were chasing to impress people who don't matter.

You're left with a few essential questions:

Why do I exist?

What gives my life meaning?

What do I have of significance to contribute?

Despair dissolves your false purposes. The titles, the image, the achievements—all the things you used to measure your worth—start to look pretty damn empty. And in that dissolution, painful as it is, space opens.

It's the space for what's real. Space for the values that are yours, not inherited. Space for a purpose that comes from within, not from others. And if you resist the urge to immediately fill that space with new distractions—new goals, new projects, new addictions—something deeper begins to happen.

You develop the capacity for real self-compassion. You begin to understand the pain in others because you've met your own. You stop theorizing about suffering and start recognizing it in your bones.

That's when you discover your own agency again.

Even when you can't change what happened to you, you can choose your response. You can choose what it means.

That's what Viktor Frankl meant when he wrote:

"When we are no longer able to change a situation, we are challenged to change ourselves."

Danny's story taught me something I wish I'd never had to learn: Meaning isn't found in comfort, achievement, or stability. Meaning shows up in the places that break you open. In the moments that demand a deeper answer than the one you've been living with. In the pain you don't want, the responsibilities you didn't choose, and the suffering you'd give anything to undo.

Meaning also shows up in what you do with that pain, in how you rise, in who you become, and in how you choose to use your story.

And here's the hard truth every man eventually faces: Something in your life will call you to find a deeper meaning. The only question is whether you'll answer.

That's what this dimension is about. Not avoiding your suffering, numbing it, or outrunning it, but learning how to turn it into direction and strength, the kind that doesn't get blown away when life hits you from the blind side.

Over time, little by little, my trauma, grief, and loss somehow began to mature. Still painful, still missing Danny, and longing to turn back time, but forging my life forward with meaning and gratitude for what I could contribute changed me in ways I could not have imagined.

Meaning isn't discovered. Meaning is forged. And often, that forging happens in the fire you'd never choose, but somehow survive.

INNER WORK SECTION

NOTES

THE WORK (Grab your journal!)

Viktor Frankl discovered that those who maintained a sense of meaning—even in unimaginable horror—had the strongest chance of survival. The question now is: what gives your life meaning?

Start by writing your answer to these three fundamental questions:

1. Why do I exist?
2. What gives my life meaning?
3. What do I have of significance to contribute?

Don't overthink it. Write whatever comes up, even if it feels uncertain or incomplete.

Now, think about a time of crisis, grief, loss, or despair in your life—a moment when you questioned whether anything mattered. Write about that experience. What did you lose? What fell apart? How did it change you?

Looking back at that painful period, what meaning eventually emerged from it? Did it clarify what truly matters to you? Did it dissolve superficial goals and reveal authentic aspirations? Did it deepen your compassion or connect you to a larger purpose? If meaning hasn't emerged yet, what would it take for that suffering to become part of a larger narrative?

Frankl taught that we can discover meaning in three ways:

1. Through purposeful work or creating something of value
2. Through experiences and encounters with others (particularly love)
3. Through our attitude toward unavoidable suffering

For each of these three pathways, write about where you're finding meaning now—or where you're not finding it and need to.

Finally, answer this: What is your why? Frankl wrote that "those who have a 'why' to live can bear almost any 'how.'" What is the "why" that will carry you through the hard times ahead? What purpose feels so true that you know you were meant to pursue it?

If you don't have a clear answer yet, write about what you're searching for. The search itself is part of the journey.

If what has held you back is simply too painful and raw, focus on the other nine dimensions and see if this loosens the soil around the dimension of meaning.

Remember that meaning isn't something you find once and for all. It's something you discover and create continuously throughout your heroic journey.

THE FOURTH HEROIC DIMENSION:

PURPOSE

Direction, organization, and a plan of execution for actualizing what gives meaning to your life

"To find our courage and purpose, we must find something greater than what we fear."

—Gladys Arnold

What Purpose Actually Is

For the longest time, I thought meaning and purpose were basically the same thing. Two words for the same concept.

Man, was I wrong.

Understanding the difference between these two transformed how I began to approach my entire life. Similarly, once you get this distinction, you can stop wandering and start building something that actually matters.

Meaning answers: "Why was I born? What am I here to do?"

Purpose answers: "What is my plan? How do I actually do and put into action what brings meaning to my life?"

In other words, meaning is the destination. Purpose is what gets you there.

After Danny died, I discovered my meaning, which was to help people who are suffering, like those coming home from war. That realization gave me direction, but meaning alone wasn't enough. I needed purpose to turn that meaning into reality.

My purpose became building frameworks to help men rebuild their lives during crises and transitions, such as creating Men Harvesting Wisdom; writing, publishing, and narrating my first book, Transitioning Veterans: How We Get in Our Own Way, and What to Do About It; writing and publishing my second book, Be the Dawn in the Darkness: The Relentless Pursuit of Becoming Who We Are Meant to Be.

Now, decades of sitting with guys in their darkest moments have allowed me to write this work, sharing tools men can use to navigate from breakdown to breakthrough—and they're the very same tools I discovered and used to put the pieces of my own life back together.

That's how I fulfill my meaning. That's my purpose in action.

See the difference? One is the "why." The other is the "how."

Where Purpose Really Comes From

Purpose isn't something you discover fully formed, like finding buried treasure. Purpose reveals itself gradually through lived experience. It emerges at the intersection of a few key things. In fact, the Japanese have a concept called "ikigai"—your reason for being. They say it exists where four things overlap:

1. What you love

THE FOURTH HEROIC DIMENSION: PURPOSE

2. What you're good at
3. What the world needs
4. What you can be paid for

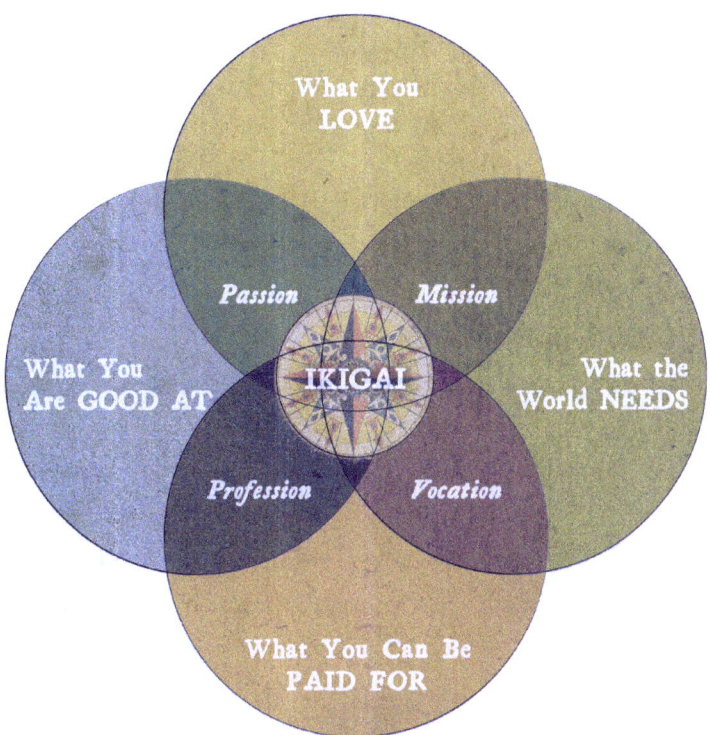

At the intersection of these four circles is something sustainable that doesn't just feel good in theory but actually works in practice. I've also found that the fourth one ("What you can get paid for") isn't 100% necessary if you make a good living at your day job and can ask for nothing in return when giving your time and gifts to help others.

Oftentimes, men (especially Veterans) give me the stink eye, wondering what I want in return for helping. Some have straight-up asked, "What do you want from me? Why are you being nice to me?" Eventually, they realize I mean it when I say

I honestly need nothing in return. If anything, I ask the same thing of them that I'm asking of you, reading this book:

Pay it forward. What you learn can help others.

But if you're not in that situation and you do need to find something you can be paid for, that's valid too. Look at how you make a living and how you build financial security. There is power in recognizing how to manifest our gifts. If you can discover what you can do or create in the world that fits this ikigai model, you will be paid in direct proportion to your ability to improve the lives of others.

What Brings You Alive (And Why That Matters)

Purpose doesn't show up with a lot of noise. It shows up as a pull, like a quiet, persistent force that keeps steering you toward the same kinds of people, problems, and places. In my experience, it often emerges in the aftermath of suffering, the way a ship adjusts course as the captain learns the winds and tides.

So, where do you naturally gravitate? What problems do you actually want to solve? What would you do even if nobody paid you?

For me, it kept coming back to helping men navigate crises. Even before Danny's passing, I was volunteering with at-risk Veterans and sitting with guys and their significant others who were struggling with transitions. I just kept being drawn to that service, and now I know that pull was telling me something about my purpose.

Purpose surfaces in the spaces where you lose track of time and where you sense this deep resonance between who you are and what you're doing. Those moments are clues, but guys often ignore them because they're too busy chasing what they think they're supposed to want. They choose careers based on what pays well, what their father did, or what seems impressive.

And those guys wake up at fifty, realizing they've built a life around someone else's definition of success.

Your Unique Combination of Talents

Purpose extends beyond self-interest. It should make you happy, yes, but more than that, it's about what you can contribute using your unique combination of experience, skills, and perspective. Nobody else has exactly what you have. Your specific blend of talents, your particular history, your way of seeing the world—none of that stuff is random. They're all pieces of your purpose.

I couldn't have built the Ten Heroic Dimensions framework I'm sharing with you today without my specific background. The Marine Corps taught me about identity, mission, meaning, and purpose. My career as a behavioral assessment analyst gave me tools to understand human patterns. Losing Danny gave me compassion I couldn't have developed any other way. All of it came together to equip me for this specific work.

What's your unique combination? What experiences have shaped you that could now serve others? Sometimes the hardest shit you've been through becomes your greatest qualification for your purpose.

Living Your Purpose Requires Authenticity

All of that said, it's one thing to understand your purpose on paper. It's another thing entirely to live it on any given weekday afternoon where you're exhausted, scared, or doubting yourself. As I mentioned before, you can't do all this work in your head. You have to live your purpose through courage, authenticity, and daily action, or else it just dies as an idea.

But that kind of vulnerability is terrifying for a lot of guys. We'd rather stay safe in roles that don't quite fit than risk being seen fully and possibly rejected—and our upbringing, culture, and society have all had a hand in moments where we've tried to show up authentically and been rejected. As I've mentioned before, those negative experiences may not have been our fault, but doing something about them now to heal and persevere is our responsibility.

Your purpose can't manifest through a bullshit version of yourself. It requires the real you—the one with specific passions and quirks and convictions that don't fit neatly into conventional boxes.

When I first started doing this work, I was worried about being too direct, too raw, too unconventional. What if people thought I was too intense? What if my approach didn't fit the typical self-help mold? What if the fact that I'm not an academic with a degree will discredit me? What if people see right through me as an imposter? Who am I to help men pull themselves through the knothole?

But the more authentically I showed up, the more the work resonated with the men who needed it.

Purpose Evolves (And That's Okay)

Your purpose isn't static. It grows as you grow. It shifts when life breaks you open and shifts again when you rebuild.

In my early twenties, I thought my purpose was being an ass-kicking Marine. Later, I believed it was becoming a successful behavioral assessment analyst. When Danny came home from war, my purpose shifted toward helping him rebuild. After he died, it changed again into helping other men navigate the same darkness he faced.

Now that I've stepped back from one-on-one work with men, my purpose has expanded into creating frameworks, writing, producing audiobooks, and building a broader mission that can reach men I'll never meet.

Each phase built on what came before. The expression changed, but the essence of service, compassion, and helping others navigate hardship remained the same.

What emerged from my work with men was a simple sense of purpose and mission:

Save lives. Help men thrive. Keep families together.

So, let me say this clearly:

Don't make the mistake of believing you must find one perfect, permanent purpose. Purpose becomes clearer as you gain experience, self-knowledge, and yes—I'm going to say it—self-love.

Courage and Self-Love

I'm not talking about soft, fluffy, and fake social media "self-love" posts. Speaking from experience, I'm talking about the self-love forged through hardship. Self-love is an expression of courage that empowers you to create a safe, fortified inner perimeter. There, you can finally set down your armor, your shield, and your sword long enough to breathe, heal, and recover.

If you're reading this book, it means your flame wasn't extinguished. Somewhere in you—beneath the pain, the numbness, the exhaustion—lives a spark. It's a glimmer of hope that says, "I can still build something meaningful."

That spark matters. This is wisdom harvested from your own life, the kind you'll pass to the men who come after you.

And that's where purpose comes in. It's why purpose and courage are heroically intertwined. If you fear being vulnerable, good. That fear is pointing directly at the work you need to do.

If you knew exactly what to do, you'd already be doing it.

And if you have figured some of this out already, then maybe your next purpose is to turn around and teach what you've learned to someone who's still in the dark.

Your Pain as Purpose Material

No matter who you are, you've probably been carrying heavy rocks in your rucksack, like grief, loss, shame, heartbreak, and failure. Some of those rocks represent people you've lost, and some represent moments that nearly broke you. You can't just throw shit like that away.

But you can transform it.

You can take those rocks and reshape them into something you carry with honor. Something that gives your life direction instead of dragging you down.

If you want to start somewhere, take a good look at whatever you've been carrying and acknowledge your pain. Name it. Write it. Speak it aloud and talk to someone you trust. Let it surface and begin the release.

Because here's the thing: When your inner demons feel your willingness to heal, to learn, and to grow, they stop clawing at your heart and start meeting you where you are. They transform into messengers instead of tormentors.

Real Integration of Purpose

Purpose is found in ordinary days, not big, wild dreams. It's in the projects you say yes to and the ones you stop pretending you'll ever complete. It's in the conversations you initiate, the company you keep, what you're willing to sacrifice, and what you refuse to compromise.

Be brutally honest with yourself. If you say your purpose is to be present for your family, but you're working sixty or eighty-hour weeks and missing the moments that matter, you don't have that purpose. You have a story you're telling yourself.

Purpose requires integration. It's your ikigai along with daily action: small, consistent steps that move you toward fulfilling your meaning.

Look at Your Origin Story

Simon Sinek is right: Your purpose is almost always rooted in your deepest experiences.

What shaped you? What broke you? What rebuilt you? There are tons of clues buried in your past. Study them, because somewhere in those moments lie pieces of your purpose.

At the same time, pay attention to the moments when life feels like you're moving with the current instead of fighting against it. That alignment isn't an accident. It's your inner self telling you that you're facing the right direction.

Your purpose serves as an integrating force for your identity, your values, and your meaning. It points toward action. And when your purpose is clear, decisions become simpler. You know which aspects of your conditioned self to embrace and which to release. You know where to focus your limited time and energy. You know what trade-offs are worth making and which ones violate your core.

Purpose doesn't eliminate the struggle, but it does give the struggle direction and significance. For me, every hard conversation I have with a man in crisis, every revision of these frameworks, and every moment spent clarifying these concepts all serve my purpose. And knowing that makes the difficulty worthwhile.

You Have to Try Things

You can't find your purpose from a safe distance. You figure it out by doing things, by trying new things that feel aligned but scare you, and by paying attention to what brings you alive and what drains you. This is especially true when you observe how your gifts and service to others impact those around you in positive, uplifting ways.

Clarity comes from engagement, which means taking action, experimenting, screwing up, refining, and trying again.

For me, the breadcrumbs were always there. A lifetime of pain may have wounded me, but it also sharpened me and tuned my inner radar. It gave me the empathy to sense another man's pain before he has words for it—not because I'm special, but because I've carried similar burdens and eventually learned how to set them down.

When you stay present, your future becomes something you can shape. I'm still learning to harvest the wisdom from my past to be present here and now. And the more I harvest, the clearer my path becomes.

Small Purposes Matter

Most people's purpose isn't world-changing or movie-worthy. That's okay. Most likely, your purpose is rooted in being a better dad, husband, son, friend, teacher, mentor, or leader.

So what if your purpose isn't to start a movement or revolutionize an industry? Your purpose might be to be a steady, reliable presence in your family when everything else is chaos. Maybe it's doing honest work that supports people you care about. Maybe it's being the guy at your job who actually gives a shit about doing things right. That kind of purpose matters. Immensely.

I've met men whose purpose was coaching Little League teams for twenty years. Men whose purpose was running a small business that employed people in their community. Men whose purpose was to be sober so their kids had a parent they could count on.

None of those sound particularly special or unique, but to the kids they coached, the employees they supported, the children who grew up with a stable father? It was everything.

Your purpose doesn't need to be impressive. It needs to be real.

Your Unique Contribution

Nobody else can fulfill your purpose. That's not motivational bullshit—it's logistics. Your specific combination of gifts, experiences, and perspective positions you to contribute something that only you can contribute.

The world needs what you have. Not a generic version of you or a sanitized version that fits expectations. The real version, with your specific abilities applied to what needs doing.

Your purpose is the unique contribution only you can make to the world around you. Finding it requires introspection and action—listening to your inner voice while engaging fully with the world, remaining open to possibility while pursuing what already brings meaning to your life.

When You Don't Feel "Special"

"That's great, John, but I'm not special. I'm just a guy trying to get through the week. I don't have some unique gift the world is waiting for. I'm a cog in the machine—one of a million, not one in a million."

I've heard that exact sentiment from many men sitting across from me. Hell, I've felt it myself, and I'm not going to insult your intelligence by telling you that you're secretly extraordinary and just don't know it yet. That's not what this is about.

Purpose doesn't require you to be exceptional. It requires you to be present.

When Danny was sitting in that frigid ditch smoking cigarettes and barely holding himself together, he didn't feel special. He felt broken. Replaceable. Like the Army had chewed him up and spit him out, with dozens of other guys to promote and fill his spot.

Here's what I told him then, and what I'm telling you now: Your purpose isn't about being the only person who could possibly do something. It's about being the person who actually shows the hell up to do it.

The Mathematics of Mattering

Let me break down why the "I'm just ordinary" argument doesn't hold up.

Yeah, there are billions of men in the world, and yes, someone else could probably do a version of what you do. But nobody else is in your specific position, with your specific relationships, facing your specific circumstances right now.

You might not be the only person who could mentor a struggling kid or another man in need, but you may very well be the only one right now who's actually willing to do it. You might not be the only person who could help your aging parents, but you're their son, and you're here. You might not be the only person who could build that business or create that art or show up for that friend, but you're the one who's actually doing it.

Let go of the cosmic sense of purpose, like it's "supposed" to be something that makes you irreplaceable in the cosmic sense. Real purpose is about being irreplaceable in the immediate, tangible, today sense to the people in front of you in the moments that are actually happening.

The Dangerous Comfort of "I'm Nobody Special"

Believing you're ordinary and "therefore purposeless" is comfortable. It lets you off the hook. If you don't believe you have a unique contribution to make, then you don't have to risk trying. You don't have to face potential failure. You can stay small and safe.

But that comfort will kill you. Maybe not physically, but it'll kill the part of you that's capable of mattering. The part that could contribute something. You don't need to believe you're special. You need to act as if your actions matter, because to someone, somewhere, they do—even if that someone is just the future you, looking back and grateful that you from today didn't give up.

What If You Still Don't Know?

What if you don't feel drawn to anything in particular, and nothing brings you alive? What if you're just trying to survive?

That's okay. You're not broken, you're just in a different phase. Sometimes we have to build stability before we can discover purpose. Sometimes we have to heal before we can contribute.

A man can rebuild his entire life starting from exactly that foundation. I've seen it, and I've lived it. Many times. Purpose reveals itself gradually as you keep moving.

If you don't have a purpose, make your first goal finding your purpose. And if you need it, you can use this purpose for today: Take care of the basics. Do the next right thing. Keep yourself alive and moving forward.

Abdication

Abdication is the act of formally giving up or renouncing a position of power or responsibility. It's abandoning any significant duty or responsibility.

Your purpose might be huge or it might be humble. But the absence of purpose—the passive drifting through life believing nothing you do matters—is not humility. It's abdication.

And no matter what you do, the work remains.

Whether you believe you're uniquely gifted or utterly ordinary, the work is the same: pay attention to what needs doing, move toward it, and contribute.

Remember: You don't need to be one in a million. You just need to be one who shows up.

INNER WORK SECTION

NOTES

THE FOURTH HEROIC DIMENSION: PURPOSE

THE WORK (Grab your journal!)

You've explored what gives your life meaning (the why). Now it's time to clarify your purpose (the how)—the specific way you'll express that meaning through concrete action and contribution.

Start with the ikigai framework. Draw four overlapping circles and label them.

Fill in each circle with as many answers as you can. Don't filter or judge—just write.

Now look at where these circles overlap. What sits at the intersection? That's where powerful clues about your purpose live.

Next, answer these questions:

1. **When do I feel most alive?** Write about the moments when you lose track of time, when your work feels like play, when you sense a deep resonance between who you are and what you're doing.

2. **What broke me open?** What experiences changed you? What parts of your pain have taught you something important? What did you survive that someone else is struggling with?

3. **What pulls me back again and again?** Think about people you naturally help, topics you never get tired of, and problems you can't ignore. These things that pull you aren't random.

4. **What am I naturally good at?** Think about your specific combination of talents, experiences, passions, and values. What can you offer that no one else can in quite the same way?

5. **Where do I feel the most aligned?** Remember that alignment is direction. Consider moments where life feels smoother. What are the times when your val-

ues and actions match and situations where you feel grounded and whole?

6. **If I stopped hiding, numbing, or playing small, what would I be willing to try?** Consider the things you're doing to avoid your purpose and what you could do if you tore down those barriers and stopped those behaviors.

Now, review everything you've written. What patterns stand out? Identify the themes you see.

Write your purpose statement. Keep it simple and action-oriented. It should answer: "I am here to _____."

Here's mine again:

"I am here to save lives, help men thrive, and keep families together."

Pretty fucking simple, right?

As I've said before, don't expect perfection. It doesn't matter if your purpose right now is "I am here to feed and walk my dog." This is version 1.0. Your purpose will evolve as you grow, but its essence will remain.

Finally, write down three concrete actions you can take this week that align with your purpose. Purpose without action is just philosophy. Make it real.

THE FIFTH HEROIC DIMENSION:

SELF-CARE

Maintaining and improving your physical, emotional, spiritual, and financial well-being

"If your compassion does not include yourself, it is incomplete."
—Jack Kornfield, *Buddha's Little Instruction Book*

It's a shame that you and I both know that too many men might see the word "self-care" in this chapter title and feel compelled to skip it entirely.

I get it. The term has been hijacked by social media influencers selling bubble baths and taking pictures of fancy meals. It sounds soft and indulgent, like something men shouldn't need if they're tough enough.

Well, that's all bullshit.

Here's what self-care actually is: maintenance. You maintain your car so it doesn't break down on the highway. You clean your weapons so they work when it matters most. You maintain your tools so they work when you need them. You maintain your living space so you don't get roaches and rodents. Self-care is the same thing- maintaining yourself—your body, your mind, your spirit, and your resources—so you don't break down when life demands the most from you.

And if you think you don't need maintenance? Look around at the men in their fifties and sixties who are falling apart. Diabetes. Heart disease. Divorced. Estranged from their kids. Broke despite decades of work. That's what happens when you ignore maintenance for forty years.

When your tank's on empty, it doesn't matter how hard you hit the gas. You won't get anywhere.

Self-care isn't optional, and like the other nine dimensions in this book, it's also heroic.

You can have the clearest vision in the world, but if your body's breaking down, your emotions are wrecked, you're spiritually empty, and your finances are a mess, you won't have the capacity to execute on any of it. Your purpose will just become something you think about instead of something you can realistically sustain.

So, let's talk about the four elements of self-care that actually matter.

Physical Self-Care: Your Foundation

Your body is the vehicle through which you experience everything. When it's not functioning well, everything else suffers. You can't think clearly when you're exhausted. You can't regulate your emotions when your blood sugar's crashing. You can't show up with energy and presence when you're carrying an extra fifty pounds and your joints ache.

In the past, I actually knew what to do to take care of myself, but I wasn't acting on it.

I had no idea how my significant childhood, adolescent, and adult trauma—along with the accumulated chronic stress I'd normalized—would exact a hefty toll over the six decades of my life.

Without going into details, no matter what your age, the next time you get your bloodwork done, ask that they check your C-reactive protein (CRP) levels, and get a coronary plaque scan. Make sure you also take note of another score, your A1C, to know your consistent blood sugar level.

Trust me, you'll want to know this information about your physical health, especially if you have had significant trauma in your life. Chronic stress corrodes and deteriorates our nervous system with almost no conscious symptoms.

If you have high CRP levels, a high coronary plaque score, and high blood sugar, your doctor will likely refer you to have an angiogram to measure soft plaque. If this is also high, find a cardiologist who specializes in these coronary health conditions.

Since learning my scores, I've made some major adjustments to my diet and lifestyle for the better. Food tastes better, and I am constantly weeding the garden of activities and projects that do not bring me joy. Mobility training and dynamic body movement are also quickly finding their way into my day because now they've become a priority.

But I'm not here to lecture you about what you already know. You know you should move your body regularly. You know you should eat food that actually fuels you instead of just temporarily satisfying cravings. You know you need sleep—real sleep, not passing out in front of the TV from too much alcohol or scrolling your phone until 2 a.m.

That's heavy, I know. But men need the truth without sugarcoating it. And before you think this is turning into a medical lecture, let's shift to something every man can relate to: our relationship with the word "exercise."

The famous comedian Bob Hope once said, "Whenever I feel like exercising, I lie down until the feeling goes away."

For me, the word "exercise" still takes me straight back to the Marines, especially when I was preparing to go to parachute jump school. Marines are not allowed to fail jump school. I wasn't about to fail, and in the six months prior to heading to Fort Benning, every morning at 4:30 a.m., freezing rain, snow, or shine, all who were training for jump school went through the following:

1. Twenty dead hang pull-ups
2. Max sit-ups in ninety seconds (at least sixty)
3. Run four miles in boots and utilities in less than thirty minutes
4. Endless pushups

After completion, we fell into formation at 7 a.m. to train with the entire company, consisting of lots more pushups and exercises, typically followed by a ten to twelve-mile run.

Before joining, I wasn't much of an athlete. The only time I ran full out was when bullies and gangs were chasing me. After joining, I learned to absolutely hate the word "exercise," mostly because I hated exercising in the extreme cold and the hot, humid, sticky, bug-infested regions of the world.

But here's the funny thing, I also discovered that I love dynamic body movement and mobility rituals: stretching, kettle bells, yoga, and qigong. Just thinking about it makes me want to stretch and move.

Funny how words work, right?

All I did was change my association with how I'm caring for my physical body. The fact is, I love being lean, flexible, and strong. These are the qualities within myself I enjoy, not the act of exercising. Going all-in, I found that for me personally, I can best keep up the practice by leading a morning mobility ritual via Zoom with a few accountability partners, which allows me to model this out for others.

The point is, don't get caught up on a word or your perception of something. Adapt and expand your thinking, reframe it into something that has motivation and juice.

Overall, for a lot of the guys I've met and worked with, the question isn't what to do but why aren't you doing it? And the answer usually comes down to one of four things:

1. **You're avoiding something.** Movement and good nutrition require you to be present in your body. If there's pain or discomfort or old trauma stored there, numbing out with food, alcohol, or sedentary behavior feels safer than actually inhabiting your physical self.

2. **You've convinced yourself you don't have time.** You have time for what you prioritize. If your physical health isn't a priority, that's a choice—and it's probably costing you more time in the long run through illness, fatigue, and decreased productivity.

3. **You don't think you're worth the investment.** This one's deeper. If you don't fundamentally believe you deserve to feel good in your body, you'll sabotage every attempt at physical self-care. This usually ties back to the conditioning we talked about in the Identity dimension.

4. **You don't have a system.** Motivation is unreliable as hell. Systems—routines, habits, structure, accountability—are what carry you when discipline wavers. If you don't have a simple system for movement, sleep, nutrition, and recovery, you'll default to old behaviors every time.

Here's what physical self-care looks like in practice: Find movement you don't hate and do it consistently. Eat food that makes you feel strong, not sluggish. Yeah, that means vegetables and stuff that comes from the earth, not ultra-processed stuff that's shipped from a factory. Sleep like your life depends on it (because it does). Get regular check-ups. Address problems before they become emergencies.

That's it. It doesn't need to be complicated, but it does need to be consistent.

Emotional Self-Care: Learning to Feel

Most men I work with are terrible at emotional self-care because they were never taught that emotions contain valuable information. They were taught to suppress, ignore, and power through.

The fact is, our emotions aren't the problem. Our relationship with our emotions is the problem.

Remember those protective parts we talked about in the Identity dimension? A huge part of their job is managing your emotional experience. The controlling part keeps you from feeling vulnerable. The angry part keeps you from feeling hurt. The people-pleasing part keeps you from feeling rejected.

Emotional self-care is learning to recognize and work with your emotions instead of being hijacked by them or numbing them out.

This means:

1. **Naming what you're actually feeling.** Most guys can identify "fine," "stressed," or "pissed off." That's not enough granularity. Are you anxious? Disappointed? Ashamed? Overwhelmed? Resentful? The more precisely you can name it, the more you can understand what it's telling you.

THE FIFTH HEROIC DIMENSION: SELF-CARE

2. **Having outlets for emotional energy.** Emotions are energy in motion. They need somewhere to go. Maybe that's talking with someone you trust. Maybe it's intense physical activity. Maybe it's journaling. Maybe it's crying in your truck in the parking lot—yeah, you read right: crying. Whatever it is, the energy needs to move through you, not get stored in your body or blasted at people who don't deserve it.

3. **Setting boundaries.** Emotional self-care includes protecting yourself from people and situations that consistently drain you or violate your needs and values. You don't have to stay in relationships that deplete you, but before ending them, maybe consider how you are contributing to the depletion. You don't have to say yes to every obligation. "No" is a complete sentence.

4. **Getting help when you need it.** Therapy isn't a sign of weakness. It's a sign you're serious about doing the work. If you've got high ACEs scores, unresolved trauma, or patterns you can't break on your own, find a therapist who specializes in men's issues or trauma. It's an investment in yourself.

The hard truth is, you can't lead yourself (or anyone else) effectively if you're emotionally dysregulated. The guy who flies into rage at minor inconveniences, who shuts down when things get difficult, who medicates every uncomfortable feeling with substances or distractions—that guy is desperately in need of the Ten Heroic Dimensions but can't or won't see it until he is sick and tired of being sick and tired.

Until he's sick and tired of hanging on by a thread, this work will seem unrealistic and daunting. But when that guy wakes up and comes to his senses, look out. That said, sudden surges of motivation can be either healthy or unhealthy depending on the stimulus. Perhaps a woman he's attracted to tells him he's too fat, so he suddenly decides to whip himself back in shape—but now, he's actually self-medicating with exercise instead of actually addressing his underlying issues.

Or, maybe he needs to get some new work clothes and is faced with the reality of a 44-inch waist. To get to and maintain his goal of a 32-inch waist, he has to dig deep and find himself. Without taking that action, he's more likely to fall back to the whims and impulses of his conditioned self and all of the poor habits that come with it.

To paraphrase from Joe Dispenza, author of *You Are the Placebo* and *Breaking the Habit of Being Yourself*, (which I highly recommend reading): Your thoughts create the emotions you feel. Your emotions trigger the corresponding chemical soup that your body lives in.

If you are constantly ruminating on anger, resentment, shame, or any other negative emotion, your emotional command center instantly adjusts the chemical response within your body to obey the chemical signature of the corresponding thought.

Even impulse thoughts that last only a nanosecond are dropping depth charges into your emotional awareness that cause physiological responses in a nanosecond.

A nanosecond is fast. A nanosecond is the amount of time it takes at a New York intersection between the time the traffic light goes from red to green before the taxi drivers hit their horns.

Jokes aside, the most obvious example of a nanosecond is when a man is aroused by seeing someone he is attracted to. You see the person, and before you break a half smile, your body has already fired off the message to your chemical response department. There's a noticeable surge of arousal in your body.

Here's another example: You're driving down a beautiful beachfront road, relaxed and daydreaming, and suddenly you notice that not only is there a police car right on your ass, but its lights are flashing to pull you over. You feel a surge of panic, and your body immediately tenses.

See what I mean? These are automatic responses where thoughts hijack your emotions and body chemistry.

So, curate your thoughts mindfully as if they are going into a scrapbook of your best-imagined self. Even if your psyche doesn't fully believe your vision of your imagined self, your body obeys the commands of the emotional signature of your thoughts. Positive or negative, resourceful or unhelpful, your chemical command center is the traffic cop that's examining the emotional signatures coming at him. His job is not to judge whether your thoughts are healthy or unhealthy. He has nanoseconds to send the emotional signature to the chemical response.

Trust me, by the time you start working on just one or two dimensions that are screaming for your attention, your thoughts will begin to shift toward who you are becoming. And shortly thereafter, you may experience the qualities of ease and possibility which will help your body chemistry to calm and relax.

Spiritual Self-Care: Connection to Something Greater

I'm not here to convert you to anything.

A lot of bad things have happened throughout my life. This has left me uncertain if I will ever embrace any form of organized religion. I'm not closed to this, but my path for now is simply cultivating my own spiritual path.

But spiritual self-care isn't about a particular religion. Spiritual self-care is maintaining your connection to meaning, purpose, and the internal alignment of who you really are.

This can present a challenge for some because it forces us to slow down, sit with ourselves, and face the parts of life we can't control or fix through effort alone. It requires vulnerability, which for men is often the one thing we were never taught to tolerate (or taught never to tolerate), let alone practice.

When I was about eight, my great-aunt Glad gave me the simplest, strongest spiritual truth I've ever encountered, and I carry it with me still:

"God is love."

Her words blazed into the deepest parts of my psyche.

"You see, John, I have explored the depths of many of the world's greatest religions, and after separating the extremism in each, I discovered a universal truth that good people believe about their faith, and that is, God is love. If you find a religion you choose to devote yourself to, that is your choice. But if you simply know and believe that God is love, this will not only provide a spiritual path to follow, you will learn to appreciate and coexist with people of any faith."

I needed this advice as a young boy. Today, decades after her passing, she is the angel on my shoulder, guiding me still. God is love has been enough to anchor me through the hardest seasons of my life.

Glad wasn't bound to a doctrine. She carried a presence that made people feel accepted, grounded, and seen. It didn't matter who they worshipped, what they believed, or whether they believed anything at all. She lived from that center, and everyone felt it.

That idea followed me through decades of searching—and I do consider myself a seeker, not a joiner. I stay open, curious, and grounded in the truth Glad handed to me. I've had conversations around fire pits with Persian men, shared meals with Muslim soldiers, sat in Buddhist temples, and participated in Native American and First Nations ceremonies that cracked me open. I've seen spirituality in the quiet discipline of the

Marines I served with, the humility of a father, and the raw honesty of a man in recovery.

Different paths, different practices, and the same thread running through all of them: God is love.

For me, a single enlistment in the Marine Corps was the closest thing to religious devotion. The Marine Corps ethos—Unit, Corps, God, Country—created a sense of belonging, identity, and purpose I've never fully replicated anywhere else. To me, it was a spiritual connection of being connected to something bigger than myself.

What Spiritual Self-Care Looks Like

It's simpler than you might think:

1. **Make time for reflection.** You need space to really hear yourself, like a few minutes of stillness, prayer, meditation, journaling, or walking in nature.
2. **Find a community with shared values.** Men need other men who aren't afraid of depth, honesty, or the truth. Find a group, a circle, a mentor, or a couple of close friends who you can trust to go beyond small talk. If you are already a man of faith, you likely already have a sense of community with other men of faith, so follow your faith. If you have a low tolerance for organized religion, there are as many ways to practice spiritual connection as there are different tribes of men. The tribe of men you resonate with is out there and accessible by researching on the net. Seek and you shall find.
3. **Alignment between what you value and how you live.** When your actions don't match your values, your soul feels it before your mind does.
4. **Awe and perspective.** Experience and take the time

to appreciate moments that remind you you're not the center of the universe, like sunsets, music, drumming, service, ceremony, nature, and love.

When a man is spiritually grounded, everything else changes.

Being spiritually grounded may simply look like and feel like the love and joy you experience when beholding an innocent newborn child or baby animal. Look for what brings a sense of awe and inspiration to your awareness, and healthy thoughts will follow.

When you focus your thoughts on being emotionally and spiritually grounded, you become steadier, clearer, and less reactive. You become more intentional and connected. You stop white-knuckling your way through life and start living from a deeper place, one that supports us when effort, discipline, and willpower aren't enough.

Without spiritual self-care, everything else eventually feels hollow. So, choose one small practice and do it consistently, not perfectly. Remember that spiritual strength isn't built in leaps; it's built in rhythms.

Financial Self-Care: Freedom and Security

Now, let's talk about money, because most guys are either obsessed with it or avoiding thinking about it entirely.

Financial self-care is an area I've struggled with for most of my adult life, and I know where it comes from. When I was about fourteen, my mom lost her mind when she saw that my father's paycheck was over $2,000 for a single month. Her screams of excitement seared into my mind so completely that it created a reinforcement that I could never be better than my father. So for decades (a good part of my young adult life), I lived with a regulator on my self-worth and earning potential that constantly hovered around $2,000 per month.

THE FIFTH HEROIC DIMENSION: SELF-CARE

But there's an interesting relationship between money and self-worth. Self-worth doesn't skip rungs on the ladder. If we are emotionally dysregulated from our younger years, our scarcity mentality can last a lifetime while keeping us in jobs and professions beneath our potential.

Self-worth functions more like a ratchet; click, click, click, one at a time. For me, once I recognized and understood my self-imposed comparisons with my father, my first reaction was rage, because I could clearly see that I'd been playing small and hiding out for decades. But as I learned to convert my rage into fuel and put that energy toward my personal and professional development, my earning ceiling began to rise in direct proportion to the value I was creating for others.

Financial self-care isn't about being rich. It's about creating a healthy relationship with material resources so money serves your life instead of controlling it. (Although I did hear the first key to being successful is to make more than you spend.)

Here's what that means in practice:

1. **Financial literacy.** This one's my weakest link, but I'm improving. Understand the basics, like budgeting, saving, investing, and debt management. You don't need an MBA in finance. You need to know where your money goes, have an emergency fund, and plan for the future beyond next month.

2. **Alignment with your values.** How you earn, spend, save, and share money should reflect what matters to you. If you value family time but you're working eighty-hour weeks for money you don't need, there's misalignment. If you value generosity but you're hoarding out of fear, there's misalignment.

3. **The middle path.** Financial self-care means avoiding both extremes—neither living in a scarcity mindset

where you're constantly anxious about money, nor living in excess where you're spending compulsively to fill internal voids.

4. **Boundaries around financial decisions.** Don't let other people's expectations or judgments drive your financial choices. Don't buy shit you don't need to impress people you don't like. Don't loan money you can't afford to lose. (That said, I've learned firsthand that one of the easiest ways to get rid of "friends" who are actually parasites is to loan them money.)

5. **Generosity from abundance, not obligation.** Give because it creates meaning and connection, not because you feel guilty or pressured. True generosity comes from a sense of having enough, not from trying to prove your worth. And if you don't have money to give, you can express generosity in other ways sourced from abundance, like with your time, attention, your love, and energy.

Your relationship with money often reflects deeper patterns around security, worth, power, and freedom. If you're constantly stressed about finances despite making decent money, that's usually not a math problem—it's an internal problem about never feeling safe or enough.

Financial self-care creates material conditions that support your other dimensions of growth. It removes unnecessary stressors that derail transformation. It's one of many resources to be stewarded wisely in the service of living authentically.

The Integration Point

Physical, emotional, spiritual, and financial self-care are interconnected. Physical vitality enhances emotional resilience. When your body feels strong, you can handle emotional challenges better. Emotional clarity supports spiritual discernment. When you're not drowning in unprocessed emotions, you can access deeper wisdom. Spiritual alignment guides financial decisions. When you're clear on what matters, you stop wasting money on what doesn't. Financial stability creates space for physical and emotional care. When you're not constantly stressed about survival, you can invest in health and healing.

This integration reflects the wholeness we're pursuing through this heroic dimension, because the heroic self-leader doesn't compartmentalize—he recognizes how everything influences everything else and works toward harmony.

From Self-Care to Collective Care

As you mature in self-leadership, you start to realize that self-care is never just about you. Your well-being is directly tied to the well-being of the people you love and the world you live in.

A man who takes care of himself is far more capable of taking care of his family. You may have heard the phrase, "You can't pour from an empty cup," and it's true. You also can't protect, provide, support, or lead if you're falling apart on the inside.

It doesn't matter how you identify or what labels you use. Every man reading this knows what I mean. We were all boys once. We carry some of the same wiring. We're inextricably connected with shared instincts, vulnerabilities, and responsibilities.

A prime example of how men in our world are in trouble is that the world's superpowers are led by men who are driving us to the brink of a nuclear winter.

These primates are having a stare-down contest. And no one is blinking.

The territorial and protective nature of men, when left unchecked, only leads to the need for more power. An unbalanced man in any one area, or a combination of them, has the potential to become a danger to himself and others. But the man who's physically healthy, emotionally regulated, spiritually grounded, and financially stable has the capacity to contribute to his community and, more importantly, to a world that needs us. And make no mistake: the world does need us to come together as balanced men.

Allow Your Self-Care to Evolve with You

Now that I'm in my early sixties, I have been cultivating a healthier mindset about self-care. I no longer compete with anyone, especially myself. I've been an alpha driver all my life. I've got that down, but that has exhausted and depleted tremendous amounts of energy I can now direct toward calm and peaceful self-care.

I'm less focused on who I'm becoming because that is now taking care of itself with my work and writing. I'm focused on age ninety, which, considering how fast time has flown, doesn't seem too far off.

My intention at ninety is to have strong cognitive function, strong cardio, and to be lean, strong, and flexible. Whether I make it to ninety is questionable, but with the mindset I've cultivated, I'm enjoying my time because I make it so.

Remember, you can't lead yourself effectively if you're broken down. You can't live your purpose if you're falling apart. You can't contribute meaningfully if you're depleted. And you can't build the life you want if you keep ignoring the maintenance required to live it.

And the element of self-care you're neglecting the most? That's the one you start with.

INNER WORK SECTION

NOTES

THE WORK (Grab your journal!)

Where are you running on empty?

Take an honest look at how you're actually maintaining yourself across all four elements of self-care. Remember that this isn't about what you think you should be doing. The goal of this work is to get real about what's actually happening.

1. **Physical:** On a scale of one to ten, how physically capable do you feel right now? Not how you used to feel, not how you want to feel. How do you actually feel when you wake up in the morning, move through your day, and go to bed at night?

   What's one physical habit you've let slide that you know would make a difference if you reinstated it? Be specific. Not "exercise more" but "Walk twenty minutes every morning before work."

2. **Emotional:** What emotion are you avoiding most right now? (If your answer is "none," that's bullshit. You're lying to yourself—try again.) What would it cost you to actually feel it instead of managing it, suppressing it, or medicating it?

   Who in your life can you be emotionally honest with without having to perform or protect them? If the answer is "nobody," that's your starting point.

3. **Spiritual:** When was the last time you felt connected to something larger than your immediate concerns? Describe that moment. What were you doing? Who were you with? What made it meaningful? How long has it been since you've intentionally created space for that kind of connection?

   What's one practice—no matter how small—you could build into your week to cultivate that sense of meaning or transcendence? It could be as simple as being present and loving with your significant other, or doing a single act of kindness for another. These can be among the most spiritual of moments because they are real and authentic.

4. **Financial:** Complete this sentence honestly: "My biggest fear about money is _____." Now complete this one: "If money weren't a concern, the first thing I'd change about my life would be _____."

What does the gap between these two answers tell you about what you need to address? Is it an earning problem, a spending problem, or a mindset problem?

Now, answer the Integration Question: Of these four elements, which one is most depleted right now? Which one, if you started taking it seriously, would create the most positive ripple effect across the other areas? Then, identify one concrete action you could take this week to start filling that tank back up?

As always, don't just think about this. Write it down. The act of putting pen to paper forces clarity that thinking alone doesn't provide.

THE SIXTH HEROIC DIMENSION:

ROLES

How you move through the world and show up for the people that matter most

"The key is not to prioritize what's on your schedule, but to schedule your priorities."
—Stephen Covey, *The 7 Habits of Highly Effective People*

Your life becomes far less chaotic the moment your roles stop competing and start aligning around the man you truly are. So, what do you do when you feel fragmented?

Maybe you're a husband. A father. An employee. Maybe you've got a side hustle, or you're a straight-up business owner. Maybe you're a son caring for aging parents. A friend. A mentor. A Veteran. An uncle. A community member.

Maybe you're also the man everyone relies on—the steady one, the strong one—whether you chose that role or not.

How many hats are you wearing right now? Five? Ten?

And how many of those roles are ones you intentionally stepped into versus the ones you're just responding to because someone needs you, someone depends on you, or someone expects it from you?

Too many men are being torn apart by their roles instead of being strengthened by them. They're showing up as different versions of themselves depending on who's in the room—not because they're being strategic, but because they've lost sight of who they actually are underneath all those obligations.

You probably see it all the time in the guys in your own life, too, like the man who's a powerhouse at work but emotionally missing at home and the guy who's reliable for everyone except himself.

In your own life, maybe you rush from Work Mode to Dad Mode to Husband Mode, switching personas like you're changing channels. Or maybe you rush from First Job Mode to Second Job Mode to Friend Mode. Whatever it is, at the end of the day, you're exhausted from performing instead of just being.

You've managed to keep all the plates spinning, but you have no idea what any of it's actually for. That fragmentation can destroy us from the inside out.

The Fragmentation Test

To see if fragmentation is running your life, ask yourself three questions:

1. Am I the same man regardless of each role I am in?
2. Do I know my anchor role, or do I simply react to whoever needs me most?
3. Do my daily actions reflect my purpose or my obligations?

If any of these questions hit a nerve, you're not alone. Tons of guys are living fragmented lives without realizing it.

Signs You're Out of Alignment

There are a few unmistakable signs that your roles are pulling you in different directions:

- You're winning on paper but losing yourself.
- You're needed everywhere and nourished nowhere.
- You're living by expectations instead of intention.
- You're switching personas just to survive the day.
- You're reacting to life instead of choosing your direction.

If any of these hit hard, this isn't failure—it's awareness. And awareness is the beginning of alignment. Everything you've built internally shows up here. Your roles are how your identity moves through the world.

There was a moment in my life when I was trying to be everything to everyone and failing at all of it. I was burnt out, short-tempered, and numb, and I remember sitting alone in my car after a long day thinking, "This can't be what being a man is supposed to feel like." That moment didn't fix everything, but showed me that something had to change, and that change had to start with who I was being, not what I was doing.

When your roles compete rather than complement each other, pulling you in opposite directions instead of organizing around a center, you end up living a divided life. And a divided life is exhausting.

The False Solution: Goals Over Intentions

We need to look honestly at the traditional advice men are given about "managing" their roles.

In *The 7 Habits of Highly Effective People*, Stephen Covey teaches readers to identify their key roles and set weekly goals within each one. It's solid advice, and I used his system for years. The idea is to list out your roles (father, husband, manager, friend, whatever), then set specific goals for each role so you're not letting any area of your life go to shit while you focus on work.

Makes sense, right? Balanced attention across life areas. Nothing gets neglected.

But after decades of working with men in crisis, I've learned that this approach treats roles like separate compartments you're managing. This works for some guys, but for others, it might keep them busy without necessarily keeping them aligned.

And here's the thing: If I'm your friend, I don't have "goals" attached to our friendship. I have meaningful intentions.

Intentions resonate more naturally. They feel authentic. They connect you emotionally.

Roles Rooted in Who You Really Are

Ultimately, the problem usually isn't the roles themselves. The problem is when your roles aren't rooted in who you actually are.

If you're just performing roles—doing what's expected, meeting obligations, checking boxes—you're living someone else's script. You're the guy who looks successful on paper but feels hollow inside. All those roles you're juggling become different ways of seeking approval or avoiding pain rather than serving you or anyone around you.

Covey wasn't wrong; he just didn't go far enough.

Goals help you manage roles.

Intentions help you align them.

The True Solution: Intentions

An intention is how you choose to show up, regardless of whether you hit a specific outcome. It's a direction, an orientation, a commitment to a way of being.

There's nothing wrong with goals. They're useful. But goals focus on achievement. You either meet them or you don't. It's binary—pass or fail.

Intentions work differently. An intention is how you choose to show up, regardless of the outcome. It's an orientation and a commitment to a way of being.

As a husband, your goal might be "have a date night with my wife." Your intention is "be fully present when I'm with her."

See the difference?

The goal can be met by physically showing up, while the intention requires your heart, not just your body.

In other words, goals tell you what to do. Intentions tell you how to be. And when you're clear on your intentions, the right goals emerge naturally. Without clear intentions, you end up achieving things that don't actually matter.

Integration: When Roles Work Together

Intentions create alignment, and that integration ensures your roles strengthen and reinforce each other instead of competing.

After Danny's passing, when I got clear on my identity and purpose, suddenly my roles weren't fragmented anymore. They were expressions of the same thing.

When I understood how to channel my pain and suffering, my relationships began to heal. Eventually, they thrived because I finally had balance, and that gave me energy.

In this work, you will begin to experience brief flashes of passionate, sustainable clarity—moments when everything aligns, and you feel unmistakably connected to who you are and what matters. Over time, those flashes linger longer. Eventually, they become your new normal.

For me, this shift required a constant awareness of my self-care and mindset. I still get triggered into dark places, but I no longer take the bait or sink into them. I see the trigger, I breathe, and I choose a different response.

What Integration Feels Like

Integration has a feel to it:
- Calm instead of chaos
- One man instead of many masks
- Fast decisions, fewer doubts
- Quiet confidence
- Real energy
- Nothing to hide

Integration doesn't fix everything, but it does put you back in the driver's seat. It gives you a center point to return to when life pulls at you from every angle.

Your Why Is Your Way

Let me tell you about Maral.

I met him through mutual friends on a business project. He's Turkish-born, raised in New Jersey from his teens, and has a brilliant mind he can't turn off. He's a former underwater SAT commando in Turkish Special Operations—sort of the Turkish equivalent of our U.S. Naval Special Warfare elite. He's the kind of guy who'd triple-check his gear and oxygen tanks and meticulously chart his course obsessively before he'd go underwater.

That brilliant mind blessed him with an extraordinary attention to detail, which kept him alive on dangerous missions. That superpower—velocity, precision, obsessive focus—served him well in the military. But in civilian life? It damn near killed him.

He became a globe-trotting entrepreneur with too much freedom, money, and time. He started using cocaine to work more hours and drive more results. That spiraled into addiction, and he lost his marriage, his company, and his wealth, all by his mid to early thirties. By the time our conversations got real, he was barely holding onto supervised visitation with his four-year-old daughter, Grace. He had to take a urinalysis test in front of his ex-wife before each visit to prove he was clean.

He felt hopeless and suicidal, convinced the world would be better off without him.

During one of our video calls, Maral was jumping from one complaint to the next, getting himself worked up about how everyone around him was wrong, incompetent, or incapable of understanding his genius. Nothing met his standards.

I stopped him and paraphrased my favorite Jim Rohn quote:

"Maral, there's only one problem with your list of people and things you're frustrated with: you're not on it."

Silence.

"I think your biggest problem is that you're part of the problem. But believe it or not, I think you're closer to a breakthrough than a breakdown."

He just stared at me, so then I asked him, "What's your daughter's name?"

"Grace."

His demeanor shifted, and his expression softened when he said her name. The tension in his forehead eased up, and his eyes slightly brightened.

I continued, "I've noticed that every time you talk about her, you completely relax. She seems to be the only person you're not frustrated with."

He smiled a little and gazed off. I asked him if he was there when Grace was born and if he remembered the first time she looked back at him, straight into his eyes.

"Man, that was a moment," he said, his voice dropping into something deeper and more genuine than I'd heard from him in months.

"Humor me," I said. "Imagine you could float back into that moment, right now. Take your time. See what you were seeing, feel what you were feeling, and take a slow inhale through your nose.

Let me know when you're there."

It took maybe three to four seconds. "I'm there."

"What are you experiencing?"

"Love. Pure love." His voice cracked. "I just feel this warmth in my heart."

I remained quiet as he processed the experience. He averted his gaze from me as he took in the moment. When he looked back up, his eyes were clear.

"Grace is my why," he said. "She's my purpose. She's why I was born."

What he'd just done was important. A few minutes ago, he was feeling agitated, lost, and hopeless. Now, he was in a completely different space.

I added, "You shifted your entire state by choosing where to focus your attention." Then, I quoted my great-aunt Glad and said, "When you find something greater than what you fear, you find what gives you meaning and purpose."

He sat up straighter. His jaw set.

"I need to be here for Grace."

That was Maral's moment of departure. He went from being lost to discovering his primary role—and not just what it demanded of him, but what it meant to him.

The Anchor Role

Maral didn't need to figure out ten different roles or set goals for each one. He needed one clear role that everything else could organize around. For him, it was being a father—specifically, Grace's father. That central truth solidified the Sixth Heroic Dimension: Roles, giving him clarity that took care of the First Heroic Dimension: Identity. In turn, this paved the way to understanding the Third Heroic Dimension: Meaning and Fourth Heroic Dimension: Purpose. All together, these dimensions illuminated the Tenth Heroic Dimension: Legacy, or what he wanted to leave behind for Grace.

And getting clean was no longer just part of Maral's recovery—it informed the Fifth Heroic Dimension: Self-Care and became an expression of becoming the father Grace deserved. Even his interactions with her mother changed to provide more healthy co-parenting for Grace. His work, relationships, and daily choices all began to organize around that one anchored role, which gave structure to everything else.

Like Maral, you need one primary role, rooted in identity, meaning, purpose, fueled by self-care, and illuminating your legacy. That anchor role might be being a father, a husband, or a leader doing work that serves something larger than yourself. Maybe it's being a Veteran who helps other Veterans transition home.

The specific role doesn't matter. What matters is that it's rooted in authenticity rather than in obligations, expectations, or external pressure. And when you're clear on your anchor role, your other roles stop competing and begin to support and complement each other.

Setting Intentions That Actually Guide You

So, how do you actually use intentions within your roles?

Start with your anchor role and ask yourself:

How do I want to show up in this role? Not what do I want to achieve, but who do I want to be?

For Maral, his intention as Grace's father became "Be present, steady, and emotionally available."

That's not a goal. There's no deadline, no measurable outcome. It's an orientation and a way of being that guides his choices every single day.

When he's with Grace, that intention reminds him to put his phone away, to be fully there. When he's tempted to spiral into old patterns, that intention brings him back. When he's making decisions about work or relationships or how he spends his time, he can ask: "Does this align with being present, steady, and emotionally available for my daughter?"

That's the power of a clear intention.

Now do that for your other important roles. Not all fifteen roles you're juggling—pick the three to five that actually matter. They're the ones that most deeply connect to your values and purpose.

For each role, clarify your intention, like:

1. **As a husband:** "Be emotionally honest and create safety for vulnerability."
2. **I am a father:** "Be present, receptive, and emotionally available with each child."

3. **As a leader at work:** "Bring out the best in my team through clear expectations and genuine care."
4. **As a friend:** "Show up consistently, especially when it's hard."

Again, these aren't things you achieve and check off. They're ongoing orientations that shape how you move through each day.

When Roles Conflict: Dynamic Tension Vs. Destructive Tension

Even with clear intentions, your roles will still conflict sometimes. That's life. You can't be in two places at once, and it's why understanding the difference between dynamic tension and destructive tension is important.

Dynamic tension is what makes people and teams perform at peak levels. It's the productive strain between competing priorities that forces you to grow, prioritize, and get creative. The tension between being a present father and building a career that provides for your family? That can sharpen you. It forces choices that clarify what actually matters.

Destructive tension is different. It's when meeting one role's demands requires you to violate the values of another. You feel destructive tension when there's no way to win, only different ways to lose. That tension doesn't sharpen you. Instead, it grinds you down.

The difference often comes down to whether the tension is organized around a clear center. When your roles are rooted in your actual identity and purpose, those conflicts become easier to navigate. You're not just reacting to whoever's loudest or whatever feels most urgent. You've got clarity about what actually matters.

Maral had to make choices like this constantly in his recovery. Some of his business opportunities required travel that would've taken him away from Grace during his limited visitation. Old friends wanted him to join them in environments that would've threatened his sobriety. Even legitimate opportunities that could've advanced his career sometimes conflicted with what he needed to prioritize as a father.

His anchor role and clear intention gave him a framework for those decisions. It didn't magically transform them all into easy decisions—clarity doesn't eliminate difficulty. But he wasn't paralyzed by competing obligations anymore. He knew what he was building toward.

Roles as Expressions of Identity

Your roles shouldn't fragment your identity—they should express it. When your roles are aligned with your authentic self, they stop feeling like performances. You're not managing multiple personalities or code-switching based on who's in the room. You're simply being yourself in different contexts, with different emphases, but the same foundation.

And that's when life stops feeling so damn exhausting.

Identity provides the foundation, values guide the choices, meaning gives the why, purpose points the direction, and self-care maintains the capacity.

Roles are how all of that gets expressed in your actual daily life. When they're grounded in who you really are, your roles aren't obligations but opportunities to live out everything you've been building.

A man who knows who he is doesn't get pulled apart by every role he plays. He brings the same grounded presence into each one.

Make It a Daily Practice

Living your roles with clear intentions requires daily attention. We often drift not because we lack clarity, but because we don't revisit it often enough. Here are practices that can keep you aligned:

- Morning review
- Evening reflection
- Weekly check-ins

Morning and evening are critical transition points. In the morning—before the day gets crazy—I review my primary roles and reset my intentions. "Today, I'm showing up as a husband who's present and supportive. As a mentor who's honest and direct. As a man doing this work not for recognition, but because it matters."

It takes maybe three minutes, but those three minutes orient my entire day.

In the evening, I reflect. Where did I honor my intentions? Where did I drift? When did I default to old patterns instead of conscious choice? I don't reflect to beat myself up; I reflect to learn, adjust, and try again tomorrow.

Weekly check-ins matter too. On Sunday evenings, review your key roles. Make sure your intentions still align with your values. Set specific goals if you need them—but only if they serve your deeper intentions. When you tell yourself, "Make this week count!" it becomes a manageable chunk of time to focus, recalibrate, and move forward.

This rhythm keeps you honest and prevents drift. You can have perfect clarity about your roles, but if you don't consistently check in, you'll slide back into reactive mode without even noticing.

Of course, your roles will be different from Maral's, different from mine, and different from anyone else's. But the principle holds: when your roles emerge from authentic identity and align with clear intentions, life stops feeling fragmented and starts feeling whole.

INNER WORK SECTION

NOTES

THE WORK (Grab your journal!)

Time to get clear on your roles and the intentions that will guide how you show up in them.

1. **Identify your anchor role.** What's the role that matters most to you right now—the one that connects to your deepest sense of meaning and purpose? Don't overthink this. What role, if you were failing at it, would make everything else feel meaningless? That's your anchor.

   Write it down: "My anchor role is _____."

2. **Clarify your intention for that role.** Not what you want to achieve, but how you want to be. If someone were watching you in this role at your absolute best, what qualities would they observe?

   Write your intention as a statement: "In this role, I am/I bring/I embody _____."

3. **Name your other key roles.** You don't need to list every role you play. Pick the three to five that genuinely matter—the ones connected to your values and purpose, not just obligations you're managing. For each one, write a clear intention about how you want to show up.

4. **Look for conflicts.** Where do your roles naturally compete for time, energy, or attention? Write about the conflicts that show up most often. Now, looking at your anchor role and core intentions, how might those conflicts be resolved or navigated more consciously?

5. **Check your calendar and commitments.** Look at how you're actually spending your time over the past week. Does it reflect your stated anchor role and intentions? Or is there a gap between what you say matters and how you're actually living? Be honest. The gap isn't judgment—it's information.

6. **Set one intention for this week.** Choose one role where you know you've been drifting or performing instead of being present. What's one specific intention you can set for how you'll show up in that role this week? Make it concrete enough that you'll know whether you're honoring it.

7. **Finally:** What would change if your roles stopped competing and started complementing each other? What would you gain? What would you have to let go of?

Write about the integrated life that becomes possible when everything organizes around what actually matters.

THE SEVENTH HEROIC DIMENSION:

VISION

The compelling picture of your future that organizes your choices and drives your actions

"Vision without action is merely a dream. Action without vision just passes the time. Vision with action can change the world."
—Joel Barker, The Power of Vision

Imagine it is three to five years from now.

Can you picture your life five years from now? Not the vague hope that things will be better or different. I mean a clear, specific picture of where you're living, what you're doing with your days, who you're surrounded by, and what you've built.

A lot of men can't.

They wake up tired, go to work, come home numb, and repeat. They spend their days solving urgent problems but never build anything meaningful.

Their lives are full of motion but empty of direction. They're so busy managing the present—putting out fires, meeting obligations, getting through the week—that the future is just this abstract thing that'll somehow work itself out.

And when you ask them what they want, they tell you what they don't want:

- "I don't want to be stuck in this job."
- "I don't want to feel this exhausted."
- "I don't want my marriage to keep deteriorating."

All legitimate concerns, but moving away from what you don't want isn't the same as moving toward what you do want.

Playing to not lose is different than playing to win. It's more exhausting, too.

When you lose your ability to envision a meaningful future, you lose your capacity to make meaningful choices in the present. Everything becomes reactive. Without some form of a vision of what we want and who we are becoming, it's as if we are stepping onto a raft and into the current with no oars and with no idea when we will make it back to shore. You can't build anything when you're being carried by a current you can't command.

Vision is what separates men who are drifting from men who are building something that matters.

For a lot of guys, losing vision doesn't happen all at once. It sneaks up. You don't notice it until the symptoms start showing up in your daily life. Everything starts to feel the same, you're reacting instead of choosing, you can't picture who you're becoming, and you feel tired in a way that rest doesn't fix.

The number one sign? You've stopped thinking about the future because it feels pointless or overwhelming.

THE SEVENTH HEROIC DIMENSION: VISION

When the Future Disappears

Recently, I completely lost my vision.

At the time of this writing, during 2023 and 2024, the world had endured numerous, back-to-back, particularly dark global events. I won't get into the political specifics because that's not the point. The point is, I became consumed by watching the world seemingly tear itself apart. I couldn't shake the feeling that everything I'd been building, everything I'd been working toward, was futile.

For weeks, I was glued to news coverage, scrolling my phone first thing in the morning, last thing at night. Each headline confirmed my worst fears. The 24-hour news cycle became an addiction I couldn't break, and it was slowly poisoning and souring everything, almost without my conscious awareness.

And something unprecedented happened that deepened my sadness: I could no longer envision my future.

For the first time in my adult life, the horizon completely vanished. I couldn't picture anything beyond the immediate present that I could do that mattered. And I've worked with men through some of the darkest transitions imaginable, the kind of shit nightmares are made of, so I knew what this meant. This wasn't writer's block or temporary discouragement. This was a fundamental collapse of my ability to imagine tomorrow being better than today.

I kept asking myself, "Why am I even writing this book? If the world is collapsing into chaos, what good is a book about personal transformation and self-leadership?"

The irony wasn't lost on me. Here I was, preparing to publish a book about transformational, heroic self-leadership while feeling utterly incapable of leading myself out of despair.

I've never handled helplessness well. Give me a problem to solve, a mission to accomplish, and I can function. But this sense of watching things fall apart while being powerless to intervene was crushing. All my frameworks, all my hard-won wisdom about resilience and transformation, felt pathetically inadequate.

I had to stop watching the news entirely. I had to step back from the doom spiral I'd created for myself.

And in that quiet space, something shifted.

The Question That Forges Vision

I woke up one morning and instead of reaching for my phone to check the news, thinking, "What fresh hell awaits us today?" a different question surfaced:

"What can I contribute?"

Not "How do I fix the world?" or "How do I stop bad things from happening?" Those overwhelming questions lead nowhere except deeper despair. But "What can I contribute?"—that question had traction. That question had a possible answer.

With that simple question came a surge of determination so powerful it literally lifted me out of bed. I'm not saying my sense of despair disappeared because this is the real world, and of course it didn't, but it did transform.

It turned into fuel.

Until the world actually ends, I need to act as if it won't. Completely and without reservation. Not out of naïve optimism, but out of stubborn defiance against despair. And the truth is, this isn't the first time in human history that things have seemed absolutely fucking bleak.

Where would we be right now if everyone had given up during those times?

And that's how I knew there must be something I could contribute. There has to be.

THE SEVENTH HEROIC DIMENSION: VISION

In that moment, I felt Danny's presence as a driving force that had shaped everything I'd become since his death. Danny had died trying to outrun his demons, but in his final years, he'd found something worth fighting for: helping other Veterans navigate the terrifying transition from warrior to civilian. He never got the chance to completely fulfill that vision, but I had carried it forward.

I thought about my great-aunt Glad. At twenty-one, she chose to live in the heart of Paris as World War II erupted. She eventually became Canada's only female war correspondent on the European continent. She couldn't remain a spectator while history unfolded. Her identity, values, meaning, purpose, self-care, and roles—all of it made her vision crystal clear. In that clarity, she found something greater than the fear she felt at the devastation all around her: documenting truth, bearing witness, contributing what only she could contribute.

Both Glad and Danny had understood that when darkness threatens to overwhelm everything, you don't retreat into safety just hoping someone else will fix it. You are the hero you've been waiting for. You find your contribution, and you make it, regardless of whether you'll live to see the results.

I know now that my work isn't finished. It's just beginning.

That's vision. It's not wishful thinking or naïve hope. Vision is seeing a future worth building and committing yourself to building it, even when—especially when—the odds seem impossible.

What Vision Actually Is

Vision isn't goals or plans, though it includes both. Vision is a compelling picture of a future state that organizes your energy and choices right now. Where goals tell you what to achieve, and plans tell you how to get there, vision tells you why it matters.

Without vision, you're just checking boxes. With vision, everything you do connects to something larger than the immediate task.

Here's what a real vision does:

1. **It pulls you forward.** You don't have to force yourself toward it because the vision itself generates energy. It's compelling enough that you want to move toward it even when the path is difficult.
2. **It organizes your choices.** When you're clear on your vision, decisions become simpler. Does this opportunity move you toward your vision or away from it? Does this relationship support where you're going or pull you off course?
3. **It provides meaning during difficulty.** The hard times—and there will be hard times—become bearable when they're in service of something you've chosen. Viktor Frankl's insight applies here: people who can connect their suffering to a meaningful future demonstrate more resilience than those who can't.
4. **It evolves with you.** Vision isn't static. As you grow, as circumstances change, as you gain clarity about who you're becoming, your vision adapts. But the core purpose usually remains consistent even as the specific expression shifts.

Vision Built on the Previous Dimensions

Your vision doesn't emerge from thin air. It grows directly from the work you've already done in the previous dimensions.

- **Identity gives you the foundation.** You can't build a meaningful vision on a false version of yourself. Your vision has to be rooted in your authentic identity—who you actually are underneath all the conditioning and adaptation.

- **Values provide the boundaries.** A vision that violates your core values will always feel hollow, no matter how impressive it looks on paper. Your vision has to align with what genuinely matters to you.
- **Meaning supplies the "why."** Your vision should connect to what gives your life significance. It should answer the question "What am I here to contribute?" in concrete, tangible terms.
- **Purpose points the direction.** Purpose is your "how," and vision is the specific future expression of that how. Vision makes your purpose visible.
- **Self-care creates the capacity.** A vision that destroys your health, depletes you emotionally, bankrupts you financially, or hollows you out spiritually isn't sustainable. Your vision has to include maintaining yourself for the long haul.
- **Roles organize the expression through intention.** Your vision should honor your most important roles rather than fragmenting them. It should show how those roles work together toward something coherent.

See how this builds? Each dimension supports the next. Vision is where everything you've clarified starts taking shape as a future you're actively building.

The Difference Between Vision and Fantasy

There's an important distinction I want to make here: not every picture of the future is a vision. Some of it's just a fantasy that never translates into action.

Here's how you can tell the difference:

- **Fantasy feels good, but doesn't demand anything from you.** You can imagine yourself successful, fit, wealthy, happy, and then go back to scrolling on your phone. Vision makes you uncomfortable because it shows you the gap between who you are now and who you need to become.
- **Fantasy stays safely abstract.** "I want to be successful" is a fantasy. Vision is specific enough that you can see it, almost taste it. You know what it looks like, feels like, and requires from you.
- **Fantasy avoids the cost.** Every real vision has a price, like time, energy, relationships, comfort, and opportunities you have to say no to. Fantasy focuses on the rewards. Vision acknowledges both the rewards and the costs, and says the trade is worth it.
- **Fantasy doesn't survive contact with reality.** The moment things get difficult, fantasy evaporates. Vision gets tested by difficulty, and while it might strengthen or evolve, it doesn't just disappear when you face obstacles.

Your vision should scare you a little—not in a reckless way, but in the way that stepping into who you're meant to become always involves leaving behind who you've been. That discomfort is how you know it's real.

Creating Your Vision

How do you actually develop a vision that's compelling enough to organize your life around?

Start by getting quiet—not doomscrolling, not consuming, not filling every moment with noise and distraction. You need space to hear yourself think.

In that quiet, ask yourself five essential questions and write down the answers:

1. **What future would make all this struggle worthwhile?**

THE SEVENTH HEROIC DIMENSION: VISION

Not what sounds impressive or what you think you should want. What future, if you could see it clearly, would make you willing to endure the difficulty of getting there?

2. **Who do you need to become to create that future?** Vision isn't just about external circumstances. It's about the person you're growing into. What qualities, capacities, or ways of being does your vision require you to develop?

3. **What would you contribute that only you can contribute?** Your vision should leverage your unique combination of experience, skills, and perspective. What can you build, create, offer that flows from who you actually are?

4. **What does this future look like in specific, tangible terms?** Close your eyes and walk through a day in that future. Where are you? What are you doing? Who's with you? What have you built? The more specific you can get, the more real it becomes.

5. **What does it feel like?** Vision isn't just visual. What's the quality of your life in that future? What emotions are present? How do you carry yourself? This emotional and somatic dimension is what makes vision compelling enough to sustain you.

Testing Your Vision

Once you've articulated a vision, you need to test it against reality. Here's how:

- **Does it align with your authentic self?** Or is it another version of what you think you should want? Be ruthless about this. A vision built on borrowed desires will collapse under pressure.

- **Does it integrate your values?** Does this vision require you to violate what matters most to you, or does it express those values in tangible form?

- **Does it honor your important roles?** Or does achieving this vision require you to abandon the people and commitments that give your life meaning?
- **Does it include maintaining yourself?** Or are you envisioning a future that would destroy your health, relationships, or financial stability on your way there?
- **Does it generate energy when you think about it?** Not just pleasant feelings, but actual motivation to take action? Real vision creates what Martha Beck calls "shackles off" feelings—a sense of expansion and possibility rather than contraction and obligation.

If your vision fails any of these tests, that's useful information. Either revise the vision or dig deeper into why you're drawn to something that doesn't actually align with who you are and what matters.

From Vision to Action

Vision without action is just wishful thinking. You don't need to have the whole path figured out before you start moving.

Your vision should be clear enough that you know the general direction, but you don't need to see every step. In fact, trying to plan everything in advance usually just paralyzes you.

Instead, ask yourself: What's the next right action that moves me toward this vision?

Not the perfect action or the most impressive action. Just the next one that's actually available to you right now. Maybe it's a conversation you need to have. Maybe it's a skill you need to develop. Maybe it's ending something that's pulling you away from your vision. Maybe it's just showing up consistently for something small while the larger picture clarifies.

Take that action. Then take the next one. Vision becomes reality through accumulated small choices, not through one dramatic leap.

As you move toward your vision, the vision itself becomes clearer. You learn things about yourself, about what's possible, about what you actually want versus what you thought you wanted. The vision evolves through implementation.

That's not failure. That's how it's supposed to work.

When Vision Gets Tested

Your vision will be tested. Guaranteed.

Things won't go according to plan. Obstacles will emerge that you didn't anticipate. People will question what you're doing. You'll have moments of doubt where your vision feels ridiculous or impossible.

Some people shatter under the scrutiny of reality. The vision looks great on paper, but the moment it gets difficult, they decide it wasn't real or wasn't worth it. But difficulty isn't evidence that your vision is wrong. Difficulty is just part of the process of building anything meaningful.

Since when has life been a total cake walk? See, the question isn't whether you'll face obstacles. The question is whether your vision is compelling enough to persist through them.

And be careful with "wanting" instead of "doing."

I heard a funny story about a man who came across a lantern in the sand while walking along the beach. As he brushes the sand away, it awakens something within which makes him drop it to the ground. A giant of a genie swirls out of the bottle, towering over him, stretching and yawning.

"Thank you for freeing me," the genie says. "I've been trapped in this lantern for thousands of years. I will grant you one wish, any wish your heart desires."

The man contemplates his choices for a good while before responding, "I know what I want. I want to be wealthy."

The genie replies with a smile, "I have granted your wish; you now want to be wealthy."

As I've shared before, my visions have been tested throughout my life, constantly and recently. I've questioned whether any of it has made a difference. There have been moments when staying numb and checked out would've been a hell of a lot easier than engaging with other people's pain while processing my own.

But my vision isn't optional. It's the thing that gets me out of bed, no matter what's going on in my life or in the world. It has given my suffering purpose and reinforced my purpose in return. It's about Danny, and me, and every man who has needed someone to sit with them in their darkest moment and help them find a way forward—which is the hope of this work. I cannot physically continue working with men one-on-one forever. And I've known too many men who martyred themselves into an early grave because they could not draw a boundary to their giving.

Over time, my vision has evolved, but it has never disappeared. That's because it is rooted in something deeper than circumstances.

Living From Your Vision

When your vision is clear and you're actively building toward it, something shifts in how you move through the world.

You stop being so reactive. Other people's urgency doesn't automatically become your emergency. Opportunities that don't align with your vision become easier to decline. Criticism that comes from people who don't share your values stops landing as hard.

You develop what I call "directional clarity"—you know where you're going, even when you don't know exactly how you'll get there. That clarity creates a kind of confidence that's different from bravado or false certainty. It's just knowing your aim is true.

Your vision also becomes a filter for everything else. Relationships that support your vision get prioritized. Habits that pull you away from your vision become obvious and easier to change. Resources like time, energy, and money get allocated based on what serves the future you're building.

Having a vision doesn't mean you become rigid or single-minded. Your vision operates as a center that everything else organizes around. When you're clear on your vision, you can be flexible about your tactics.

The Generative Nature of Vision

As you pursue your vision, you'll notice that it doesn't just change your circumstances.

It changes you.

The person who achieves their vision isn't the same person who first articulated it. You grow into someone capable of sustaining what you've built. Your capacity expands. Your understanding deepens. And often, once you've realized one vision, a larger one emerges. It's not because the first one wasn't "enough," but because achieving it opened your eyes to new possibilities.

This is the generative upward spiral of vision and growth: clear vision inspires growth beyond your current limitations.

That growth expands your capacity for a deeper, larger vision. That deeper vision calls forth even greater growth, and so on.

It's not linear. It's not neat. But it's how men who transform their lives (and the world) actually do it: one compelling vision at a time, each one building on what came before.

Your Contribution

Let me bring this back to where we started: What can you contribute today? Not when everything lines up perfectly. Not when you're finally ready.

What can you contribute right now, with what you have, from where you are?

Your honest answer to that question is where your vision begins to take shape.

For me, the contribution is this framework and this work of helping men. It emerged from my darkest moments and has become the organizing principle of my life.

Your contribution will be different. Your vision will be unique to you. But the pattern is the same: find what you can offer that flows from your authentic identity, aligns with your values, expresses your meaning, fulfills your purpose, maintains your wholeness, and honors your important roles.

Then build that future. Not perfectly, not without struggle, but deliberately and with commitment.

Because the world doesn't need your fantasy. It needs your vision made real through action.

And you don't need permission to begin.

INNER WORK SECTION

NOTES

THE WORK (Grab your journal!)

It's time to get clear on the future you're building and why it matters.

Start with the present. Before you can envision where you're going, you need to be honest about where you are. Complete these sentences:

1. Right now, I'm stuck on...
2. Right now, I'm avoiding...
3. Right now, I'm tolerating...
4. Right now, what I most want to change is...

Imagine the future worth building. Set aside thirty minutes in a quiet place where you won't be interrupted. Close your eyes and imagine it's three to five years from now. You've done the work. You've made the changes. You've built something meaningful. Now, walk through a typical day in that future:

- Where do you wake up? What's the first thing you do?
- How do you feel in your body? What's your energy level?
- What work are you doing? Why does it matter?
- Who are you surrounded by? What are those relationships like?
- What have you built, created, contributed?
- At the end of that day, what gives you the deepest sense of satisfaction?

Write this down in as much detail as possible. Don't edit. Don't make it reasonable. Just describe what you see.

Identify who you need to become. That future version of you—the one living the vision—what qualities does he have that the current you is still developing? Write down three to five characteristics or capacities you need to grow into. Be specific.

Test your vision against reality. Review what you've written and ask:

- Does this align with my authentic identity (not who I think I should be)?
- Does this honor my core values?
- Does this connect to my meaning and purpose?
- Does this maintain my physical, emotional, spiritual, and financial well-being?
- Does this integrate my most important roles?

If you answered "no" to any of these, that's important information. Either revise your vision or dig into why you're drawn to something that doesn't align.

1. **Name your contribution.** Complete this sentence: "The unique contribution I can make that would bring this vision to life is _____."
2. **Identify the next right action.** Don't worry about having the whole path figured out. Just answer: What's one action I can take this week that moves me toward this vision? Be specific. Put it on your calendar.
3. **Write your vision statement.** Distill everything into two to three sentences that capture the essence of the future you're building and why it matters. This becomes your north star—something you can return to when you're making decisions or when obstacles arise.

Example: "I'm building a life where my work serves others in tangible ways while allowing me to be present for my family. I'm becoming a man whose daily actions align with his deepest values, creating sustainable success rather than performing for approval."

Keep this vision statement somewhere you'll see it regularly. Not because you need constant motivation, but because vision requires consistent attention. It's too easy to drift back into reactive mode without regular reminders of where you're actually heading.

Back-from-the-Future Thinking

Lastly, take all of the hopes and dreams of your vision out into the future, three years, five years and really get in touch with who you have become, who you have touched, and what you have accomplished.

Stir these feelings up and make them real. Multiply these feelings ten times and then stop, turn around, and look back to where you are literally right now.

Break down the milestones that must have happened along the way to get you to that future.

These milestones are your shorter, incremental stages of growth to focus your actions in the here and now.

Get clear, make a plan, establish your milestones, and then get busy executing.

THE EIGHTH HEROIC DIMENSION:

EXECUTION

The moment your life changes from intention to reality

"The secret of getting ahead is getting started."
— Mark Twain

You can read every book in the world. You can journal, reflect, visualize, meditate, and plan.

But nothing changes until you take action. And that's where so many men get stuck.

Execution is the moment your life changes from intention to reality.

You've done the work in the previous dimensions. You understand your identity, you're clear on your values, you've connected to what gives your life meaning, you've articulated your purpose, you're maintaining yourself with self-care, you've defined your roles, and you've created a vision of the future you want to build.

So why does the gap between what you know you should do and what you actually do feel so damn wide?

Dealing With Resistance

Steven Pressfield, the author of The War of Art, brilliantly calls these difficulties out as "resistance," and resistance is rooted in the craftiness of our minds. Resistance is that force that shows up strongest when you're about to do something meaningful. The more important the action, the more resistance you'll feel.

Resistance is insidious because it's rational. There will always be a good reason why now isn't the right time. You're too tired. You need more preparation. The conditions aren't optimal. You should probably do more research first.

To use myself as an example, resistance quietly whispers in my ear to take a break and go get coffee instead of writing. To go to the store because we need butter, instead of writing. To call a friend about something seemingly important that could definitely wait until later, instead of writing. Anything to avoid the discomfort of beginning.

See what I mean?

If you can, definitely order The War of Art to accompany this work. I particularly like the audiobook version because Steven narrates it himself with a casual but commanding presence. His edginess feels East Coast, but I'm not sure where he was raised, other than he was a Navy kid born in Trinidad on a naval base. He is a no-bullshit former Marine, which is why I originally added his work to my list and gave it a listen.

Resistance is why execution requires you to stay connected to your meaning, purpose, and vision from the previous dimen-

THE EIGHTH HEROIC DIMENSION: EXECUTION

sions. When resistance whispers its excuses, you need something strong to push through. If you're just executing because you think you "should," you'll quit the moment it gets hard. But when your daily actions connect to something deeper—when you remember why this task matters, who it serves, what you're building—you can override resistance and keep moving even when the path is brutal.

You can't eliminate resistance. You can only recognize it and execute anyway. The practice is simple: notice resistance, name it ("Oh, there you are again…"), and do the thing anyway. Not perfectly. Not optimally. Just do it.

Resistance loses its power when you stop negotiating with it.

If this all sounds familiar, you're definitely not alone. People get stuck here not because they don't understand the concepts—they do. Not because they don't want to change—they want to do that, too. They get stuck because they can't translate vision into consistent action. They know the destination, but they can't seem to build momentum toward it.

Welcome to the hardest part.

Everything you've clarified in the previous seven dimensions means exactly nothing if you don't do something with it. Vision without execution is daydreaming. Values without action are just nice-sounding words. Purpose without implementation is potential that dies unrealized.

Execution is where theory meets reality. It's where you find out how to make your personal transformation tangible and real.

The Gap Between Knowing and Doing

The gap between knowing what to do and actually doing it usually isn't an information problem. As I mentioned in the Fifth Heroic Dimension: Self-Care, it's rare that guys don't know they should exercise, eat better, have that difficult conversation, start that project, or make that change.

They know. They've probably known for years.

The gap is something else.

Sometimes it's resistance—that force named in *The War of Art*.

The closer you get to something meaningful, the stronger the resistance becomes. It shows up as procrastination, distraction, and self-sabotage, like suddenly needing to reorganize your garage before you can start your actual work.

But sometimes it's overwhelm. The vision is so big, and the gap between where you are and where you want to be feels so massive that you freeze. You don't know where to start, so you don't start anywhere.

Sometimes it's fear masquerading as perfectionism. If you don't start, you can't fail. If you don't execute, you can't discover that you're not capable of what you envisioned. Staying in the planning phase feels safer than actually testing yourself.

And sometimes—this was my gap, personally—it's that you've gotten so comfortable being the guy who's "working on himself" that actually transforming would require you to let go of that identity. For some of us, there's a strange security in being the perpetual student, the guy who's always reading the next book, attending the next workshop, clarifying the next intention. Executing means graduating from student to practitioner. That's scarier than it sounds.

What Execution Feels Like

Execution rarely feels like motivation. It doesn't feel like confidence, and it sure as hell doesn't feel comfortable.

THE EIGHTH HEROIC DIMENSION: EXECUTION

Execution feels like friction, not flow. It's the grind, not the glory. If you've ever lifted weights, it's a lot like those shaky, awkward first reps that don't look (or feel) heroic at all. It feels like strapping on your gear in the dark, stepping into the cold, and moving because the mission demands it—not because you feel like it.

That said, it comes with a quiet pride that only comes after you keep your word to yourself. And it does get easier, like with anything you practice, but you have to push through the discomfort and do those reps before that happens.

It's less like motivation and more like lighting a fuse: messy, gritty, loud, and unstoppable once it ignites.

The Brutal Truth About Execution

At some point, you just have to do the damn thing.

In the Marine Corps, we'd spend hours planning a mission—studying terrain, identifying objectives, anticipating obstacles, assigning roles, and establishing contingencies. The planning mattered, absolutely. But there inevitably came a moment when planning stopped and execution began. Once you were in it, you had to commit to the plan while remaining flexible enough to adapt when reality proved different from what you'd anticipated. Luckily, there were always strong and skilled leaders around me who put a boot in my ass if I needed encouragement or clarity.

That balance—commitment plus adaptability—is the core of effective execution: too rigid and you can't adjust when circumstances change; too flexible and you're just reacting to whatever comes at you without any organizing principle. That old saying, "If you don't stand for something, you'll fall for anything."

The sweet spot is having a clear enough plan that you know your next move, but not being so attached to the plan that you can't course-correct when needed.

And here's something being an author taught me: execution requires systems, not motivation.

Motivation is unreliable. Motivation gets you started on Monday morning, but abandons you by Wednesday afternoon (or sometimes Monday afternoon). Motivation works great when everything's going well, but disappears the moment you hit an obstacle.

Systems, on the other hand, don't care how you feel. Systems don't give a shit, they just execute. You don't need to be motivated to brush your teeth—it's just part of the system of getting ready in the morning and winding down in the evening. Effective execution means building systems that work whether you're motivated or not.

Breaking Vision Into Executable Steps

Let's make this practical. You've got a vision from the previous dimension, maybe it's building a business that gives you freedom and serves others. Maybe it's transforming your health and fitness. Maybe it's rebuilding your marriage. Maybe it's transitioning from military to civilian life without losing your mind.

Whatever it is, that vision might feel overwhelming when you look at the whole thing. The gap between here and there is vast. That's normal. That's why the first step of execution is breaking the vision into components you can actually act on. After decades of working with men stuck between knowing and doing, I've distilled execution down to seven essential steps.

THE EIGHTH HEROIC DIMENSION: EXECUTION

From Paralysis to Momentum in Seven Steps

1. **Define the meaningful burden you're choosing to shoulder.**

   Start by getting clear on what challenge you're voluntarily taking on. Not what you think you should do, not what would impress others, but what burden feels meaningful enough that you're willing to carry it even when it's heavy.

   This connects directly to your purpose and vision. What responsibility are you choosing to accept? What difficult thing are you saying yes to because it matters, not because it's easy?

   Be specific. Write it down.

   In my case, I became most comfortable with people, like myself, who were suffering. I was the wounded healer because I needed to move my pain. So, shouldering the pain of others felt like a natural expression of what I had to give at the time. I didn't overthink anything. I just kept taking one step forward at a time and, eventually, my pain gave me purpose, and helping others provided the willingness I needed to always continue to march.

2. **Capture all commitments currently on your mind.**

   Your brain isn't designed to hold dozens of open loops. Every unfinished task, every "I should probably…" that's rattling around in your head is draining your mental capacity for execution.

   Take twenty minutes and do a brain dump. Write down every commitment, obligation, project, or nagging thought that's taking up space. Everything from "fix the leaking faucet" to "have that difficult conversation with my brother" to "research health insurance options."

   Get it all out of your head and onto paper. It's important to clearly see what's actually on your plate versus what you think is on your plate.

3. **Identify the resistance patterns most common for you.**

   You've got patterns. We all do. These are specific ways that resistance shows up to keep you from executing on what matters.

   Maybe your pattern is procrastination through research—you need to gather more information before you can start. Maybe it's perfectionism—if you can't do it perfectly, why start at all? Maybe it's distraction—suddenly every notification feels urgent when you sit down to do meaningful work.

   Name your patterns. When you can recognize them, you can catch them in action. "Oh, there's my perfectionism talking. I'm going to start anyway."

   What are your top three resistance patterns? Write them down. Know them.

4. **Design your environment and habits to support consistent action.**

   Willpower fails. Environment wins. If you're relying on motivation and ideal timing to execute, you're fighting an uphill battle, probably an impossible one.

   Instead, design your environment to make execution easier and resistance harder. Remove friction from the actions you want to take. Add friction to the behaviors that pull you off course.

   Want to work out consistently? Sleep in your gym clothes, put your shoes by the bed, and eliminate the decisions that give resistance an opening. Want to write? Disable your wi-fi, close all tabs, and make the page the only thing in front of you when you sit down.

   Small environmental changes create massive behavioral changes over time.

THE EIGHTH HEROIC DIMENSION: EXECUTION

5. **Take extreme and unreasonable ownership of your results.**

   Remember, your results are your responsibility. Not your circumstances. Not other people. Not bad luck or bad timing. You.

   When execution fails, it's easy to point to external factors. That finger-pointing just keeps you stuck. The moment you accept complete ownership—even for things that weren't technically your fault—you take your power back.

   Bad week? What could you have done differently? Didn't hit your target? What needs to change in your approach? Got disrupted? How can you build a system that's more resilient to disruption?

   Don't beat yourself up, either. That's not the goal here. This is about maintaining agency so you can lead yourself to the life you want.

   Want to learn more about taking extreme ownership? Check out the book and audiobook Extreme Ownership by Jocko Willink and Leif Babin. Jocko lays it down from a been there, done that leadership perspective that has been tested in real life-and-death combat. I trust his work and have attended one of his "Muster" events—some of the best leadership skills building and execution I've encountered.

6. **Engage in regular deep work on vision-aligned activities.**

   Not all action is equal. You can stay busy all day and never execute on what actually matters.

   Deep work is focused, uninterrupted time on the activities that directly advance your vision. Schedule blocks of deep work—minimum ninety minutes—where you're working on your major tasks with no distractions. This is sacred time.

Don't confuse motion with progress. Deep work is where real execution happens.

7. **Maintain a growth mindset when facing inevitable setbacks.**

    You're going to fail. Not might—will. Some weeks you won't execute like you planned. Some systems won't work. Some approaches will prove wrong.

    That's not evidence you should quit. That's evidence you're in the game.

    The difference between guys who transform and guys who stay stuck is how they interpret setbacks. A fixed mindset says, "I failed, so I'm a failure." A growth mindset says, "I failed, so I learned something about what doesn't work."

    Every setback is data. Every failure is feedback. You're not trying to execute perfectly because that's not a reasonable requirement to hold yourself to. What you're trying to do here is execute consistently while learning and adjusting.

    When you hit obstacles, ask: "What can I learn from this? How do I adjust and continue?" That question is a feedback loop that keeps you in motion instead of spiraling into shame.

    Pick the first step. Master it. Then add the next.

The Execution System That Actually Works

You need some way to track whether you're executing or just thinking about executing. But tracking can become its own form of resistance if you're not careful.

I keep it simple. At the end of each week, I ask myself three questions:

1. Did I execute on my three to five weekly actions? Yes/No for each one. No grades, no percentages. Just did it or didn't.

2. What got in the way? Not to beat myself up, but to identify patterns. Was it resistance? Poor planning? Legitimate priorities that emerged? This tells me what to adjust.
3. What's one thing I learned about execution this week? Maybe I learned I need to protect my morning time better. Maybe I learned that a particular task takes longer than I estimated. Maybe I learned that certain environments make execution easier.

That's it. Three questions. Five minutes. But over time, this tracking reveals patterns that help you refine your execution systems.

Some guys need more detailed tracking—spreadsheets, metrics, data. Fine. But don't confuse tracking with execution. The goal isn't a perfect tracking system. The goal is consistent action.

The Momentum Principle

The first step is always the hardest. Not because it's the most important step, but because it requires overcoming inertia.

In many ways, physics applies to human behavior: objects at rest tend to stay at rest; objects in motion tend to stay in motion. Once you've started executing, continuing is easier than getting started was.

This is why your daily practice should begin with the smallest possible action that counts as execution. Not the biggest, most impressive action, but the smallest one that moves you forward.

Writing a book feels overwhelming to me at times. Writing for ten minutes isn't. Building a business feels impossible. Making one phone call isn't. Transforming your health feels daunting. Putting on your shoes and walking around the block isn't.

James Clear talks about this in Atomic Habits. Focus on showing up, not on achieving some ambitious outcome. The guy who commits to two minutes of meditation will meditate more consistently than the guy who commits to an hour. Why? Because two minutes is so easy that resistance can't get traction. Once you're sitting there for two minutes, you'll often continue, but even if you don't, you've maintained the system.

Momentum builds through consistency, not intensity. The guy who executes imperfectly every day will travel further than the guy who executes perfectly once a month.

Momentum Checklist

Momentum isn't magic. It's built one honest action at a time. You can even use this checklist as your daily gut check:

- **Did I take action today, or did I only think about taking action?** Thinking isn't movement. Planning isn't movement. Action is movement.
- **What got in the way—resistance, distraction, or avoidance?** Name it. If you can name it, you can beat it.
- **What small win did I create today, no matter how minor?**
- **Tiny wins compound.** They matter far more than heroic bursts.
- **What's the next smallest step I can take to keep momentum alive?** Not the perfect step. Not the impressive step. Just the next one.

Remember that execution is about doing something consistently.

When Execution Reveals Hard Truths

Execution is a hell of a truth-teller.

THE EIGHTH HEROIC DIMENSION: EXECUTION

As long as your vision stays in your head or on paper, you can maintain whatever story you want about yourself. You're the guy who's going to start that business, get in shape, rebuild that relationship, write that book. The story can survive indefinitely without being tested.

The moment you start executing, reality provides feedback. Sometimes that feedback is brutal.

Maybe you discover you don't actually want what you thought you wanted. Maybe the work required is more than you're willing to give. Maybe your capacity is less than you believed. Maybe the vision needs to change because it was built on assumptions that don't hold up.

That's not failure. That's information.

I've watched men abandon their stated vision once they started executing on it, and it turned out they were chasing someone else's definition of success. I've watched other men discover that their vision was too small—that once they started executing, they realized they were capable of more than they'd imagined.

Both outcomes are valuable. Both require execution to reveal themselves.

The point isn't to execute perfectly on your first vision and never deviate. The point is to execute, learn, adjust, and execute again. That cycle is how you discover what you're actually building.

Course Correction Vs. Giving Up

Course correction is necessary. You'll start executing and discover that your plan needs modification. Maybe a major task isn't as important as you thought. Maybe there's a better path to your objective. Maybe circumstances changed and the original plan doesn't make sense anymore.

That's also not failure.

But giving up because it's hard? That's different. That's resistance winning.

Course correction usually comes with clarity. You can articulate why the adjustment makes sense. You can explain how the new approach better serves your ultimate objective. There's thought behind it, not just emotion.

Giving up usually comes with fog. You can't quite explain why you're stopping, it just feels too hard or pointless or impossible. There's no better plan to replace the old one, just the relief of not having to execute anymore.

If you're considering changing course, ask yourself: "Am I moving toward something better, or just away from something difficult?" Be honest. The answer tells you what you're dealing with.

The Compound Effect of Small Actions

You won't see dramatic results from one day of execution. You might not even see results from one week. But execute consistently for a month, then three months, then six months, and you'll look back shocked at how far you've traveled.

Think about it financially. Saving $10 a day doesn't feel significant. But $10 a day is $3,650 a year. Over ten years with compound interest, that's real money. The principle is the same with execution.

Ten minutes of daily execution on your vision doesn't feel significant. But ten minutes a day is over sixty hours a year. That's a substantial project completed. That's a skill developed. That's a transformation realized.

In fact, for another relevant book to put on your list, consider *The Compound Effect* by Darren Hardy.

When Execution Gets Disrupted

As with the work in any of these heroic dimensions, life will disrupt your execution.

You'll get sick. You'll face a crisis. Something unexpected will demand your attention. Your carefully built systems will get thrown into chaos.

Again: This isn't failure. This is life.

What matters is how quickly you can return to execution once the disruption passes.

Don't use disruption as an excuse to abandon your systems entirely. "Well, my routine got interrupted last week, so I guess I'll just start over next month." That's bullshit. That's resistance using disruption as camouflage.

When execution is disrupted, acknowledge it, deal with what needs dealing with, and return to your system as soon as possible. Not after everything is ideal again. As soon as possible.

Missing one day doesn't mean you've failed. Missing one week doesn't mean your system is broken. But missing one week and using that as permission to miss another month? That's losing momentum.

Get back on the horse. Even if it's just one small action, even if it's imperfect, the return is what matters.

Execution Is Who You Become

Execution makes you become the kind of person who executes.

Every time you follow through on what you said you'd do, you're reinforcing an identity. You're becoming someone who keeps commitments to himself. Someone who can be counted on. Someone who doesn't just talk about transformation but actually does the work.

That identity shift is more valuable than any specific outcome. Once you become someone who executes consistently, you can build almost anything. The skills transfer. The confidence builds. The momentum carries forward.

This is why execution is heroic. You're forging yourself into someone capable of sustained, meaningful action. That transformation—from someone who knows what to do into someone who actually does it—is the beating heart of heroic self-leadership.

You can have perfect clarity about your identity, values, meaning, purpose, vision, and roles. But if you don't execute, all that clarity just makes you a well-informed spectator of your own life.

INNER WORK SECTION

NOTES

THE WORK (Grab your journal!)

Time to build your execution system and identify what's been stopping you from actually doing the work.

Identify your gap. Be brutally honest: What have you known you should do for weeks, months, or maybe years that you still haven't done? Write it down. Don't make excuses for it. Just name it.

Name your resistance. For that thing you haven't done, what form does your resistance take? Does it show up as procrastination? Perfectionism? Suddenly every other task feels urgent? You get drowsy or distracted? You convince yourself the conditions aren't right yet? Describe how resistance operates in your specific situation.

Break down your vision. Take your vision from the previous dimension and:

1. Define the meaningful burden you're choosing to shoulder.
2. Capture all commitments currently on your mind.
3. Identify the resistance patterns most common for you.
4. Design your environment and habits to support consistent action.
5. Take extreme and unreasonable ownership of your results.
6. Engage in regular deep work on vision-aligned activities.
7. Maintain a growth mindset when facing inevitable setbacks.

Design your weekly execution system. How will you track your execution? Remember, keep it simple. Maybe it's just checking off your three to five weekly actions. Maybe it's a spreadsheet if you're that kind of guy. Maybe it's a journal where you answer those three questions every Sunday. Choose a method you'll actually use.

Anticipate your disruptions. What's most likely to disrupt your execution system? Travel? Family crisis? Work demands? For your top two likely disruptions, write: "When [disruption] happens, I'll return to execution by [specific action]."

Example: "When I travel for work, I'll return to execution by doing a ten-minute morning workout in my hotel room and protecting twenty minutes for my project work."

Commit to the compound effect. Complete this sentence: "For the next ninety days, I commit to executing on [specific action] [specific frequency]. I understand I won't see dramatic results immediately, but I'm committed to staying in the game long enough for compounding to work."

Set your first check-in. Put a date on your calendar exactly one week from now. That's when you'll do your first weekly review and assess whether your system is working or needs adjustment. Make the appointment with yourself now.

Find committed accountability partners. If you want to know whether the people around you can actually hold a standard and demonstrate accountability, here's a simple test: Send them a copy of this book. Find a blank space somewhere that feels right and write:

"If you made it this far, call me. Lunch is on me."

That's it. No follow-ups. No reminders. No hand-holding.

If they don't call, they never read it, and they won't execute with you either.

You need people who don't just talk about growth but who actually show up for it because execution is contagious, but so is avoidance. Choose your circle like your life depends on it. You need men around you who will keep their word and hold you to yours. Men who move under pressure. Men who execute when it counts. Men you can trust to go to work when everyone else freezes.

Be that man. And stand with others who are.

THE NINTH HEROIC DIMENSION:

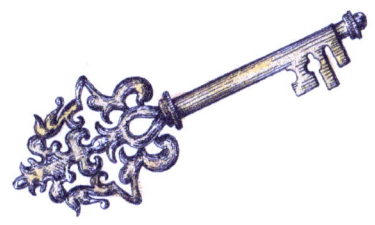

WILLINGNESS

The choice to act when everything in you says not to

"Willingness is not about being willing when we are willing, Willingness is about being willing when we are unwilling."
— Van Carrigan

You can have the clearest vision in the world, you can know your values inside and out, you can map out the perfect execution plan—but none of that shit matters if you're not willing to actually do the hard thing when it's time to do the hard thing.

Willingness is not about being willing when you are willing. It is about being willing when you are unwilling.

In Be the Dawn in the Darkness, I wrote about one of my most painful experiences of willingness. It took place several weeks into Marine Corps boot camp when I developed severe stress fractures in my shins. I was in immense, ever-increasing pain, limping badly, and struggling to keep up with the platoon on long runs. A corpsman wrapped my legs from knees to ankles in shin splints and gave me some anti-inflammatory horse pills, telling me he'd done all he could do.

The drill instructors singled me out immediately with what I can only describe as some kind of insane joy, hazing me as the weakest recruit and addressing me as a fuck-up and "Private Lamont," which stood for "Low Man on the Totem Pole." As the days of extreme physical training intensified, the bandages holding the splints would loosen and slide down to my ankles. I frequently needed to stagger-step to pull them up, which made me stand out more and more. Now, not only did I look weak—I began to feel weak. The drill instructors fed on this like vampires, sucking every ounce of motivation from me. *I'm not going to make it!* started sounding off in my head.

Within a week, I reached my limit. It happened on a long run when I fell out of formation without permission, and collapsed to the ground holding my shins. *I'm done!* exploded in my mind.

Two drill instructors towered over me. "Boy, you ready to quit? You ain't gonna make it! No way!"

The thought of my father's disappointment—the shame of going home broken to face him—jolted me to my senses. Just a shadow of a thought about my father and his look of disgust sent a massive rush of adrenaline and hate blasting through me. Enraged, I tore the shin splints entirely off both legs and stuffed them into my waistband. Within a few steps, both shins exploded as if they'd caught fire, like flesh being stripped down the entire length of both bones.

I hobbled behind the platoon for a quarter mile until I caught up. I stuffed the pain into a place deep inside myself and finished the run.

Back at the barracks, I looked at those grimy, sweat-soaked splints one last time. I hadn't been broken by the drill instructors, and I hadn't heeded my critical mind screaming for me to quit. Something triggered inside me—an urge to embrace the experience rather than escape it.

Take the pain! I let out a primal scream and dunked the shin splints into a trash can.

Take the pain became my mantra. My pain reached its excruciating peak and remained that way for another three weeks. Eventually, my damaged shins began to numb and harden. I was no longer last out of the barracks—now I was close to the leader of the pack. The drill instructors stopped taunting me and hunted for weakness somewhere else.

This is what I learned: The moment you want to quit the most is the moment willingness matters the most. And that painful experience also taught me something I've seen over and over again in myself, in Marines, and in the men I work with now: willingness isn't cinematic or inspirational. It's painful and deeply personal, and the moment you choose it—when you keep moving through pain, fear, doubt, or exhaustion—you open a door inside yourself.

The Real Enemy: Your Comfort-Seeking Brain

When fear is aroused, your survival-focused mind is designed to conserve energy and avoid threats. It doesn't care about your dreams or your potential. It cares about keeping you safe and comfortable. So, when you're about to do something hard, something that requires growth, your brain starts throwing up every excuse it can manufacture:

- "You're too tired right now."
- "You'll do it tomorrow when you're more prepared."
- "What if you fail?"
- "You don't really feel like it."

This is what I call being held hostage by your emotions. And most of us make the mistake of thinking we need to feel willing before we can be willing. That's backward. Action creates the feeling, not the other way around.

Motivation and Willingness

Motivation is emotional. Willingness is a decision.

Where motivation asks, "Do I feel like it?" willingness answers, "Do it anyway." Comfort versus choice. Unlike motivation, willingness strengthens under pressure and doesn't depend on your mood. It depends on your character.

Of course, motivation can get you started on the good days, but willingness is what carries you through the hard ones. It's like the difference between sprinting and running a marathon. Motivation is that sprint, and it's loud at the starting line, but willingness is relentless, going strong at mile twenty-nine.

In fact, David Goggins talks about willingness better than almost anyone I can recall. He says willingness is about having the conversation with yourself when you don't want to do something and doing it anyway. He calls it "callusing the mind"—you build up resistance to discomfort by voluntarily choosing discomfort over and over again.

His audiobook, *Can't Hurt Me,* is a must for every man's library.

Why We Stay Unwilling

There are three main traps I see guys fall into:
1. **The Comfort Trap:** We convince ourselves that comfort equals success. But growth lives on the other side of discomfort. Always. I've watched men stay in jobs they hate, relationships that drain them, and routines that

numb them all because the familiar discomfort feels safer than the unknown possibility of something better.

2. **The Perfectionist's Paralysis:** This one kills more dreams than failure ever could. You tell yourself you'll start when everything is perfect, when you're fully ready, when you have it all figured out. Here's the truth: you'll never be fully ready. A struggling Veteran I met years ago told me, "Not trying is safer than trying and failing." He was absolutely right about the safe part. He was also miserable.

3. **The Emotional Hostage Situation:** You make action contingent on feeling like it. "I'll work on my business when I feel inspired." "I'll have that hard conversation when I feel ready." "I'll start working out when I feel motivated." You've just handed control of your life over to temporary emotional states that change like the weather.

Building the Willingness Muscle

So, how do you actually develop willingness?

Start small. I'm serious. If you try to go from zero to hero overnight, your brain will revolt. When I first started implementing this in my own life, I used Mel Robbins' Five-Second Rule. You have an instinct to act on a goal? You have exactly five seconds to move your body toward that goal before your brain kills it.

Five. Four. Three. Two. One. Move.

Sounds stupid simple, right? It is. And it works because it interrupts that overthinking loop that breeds unwillingness.

The other thing that helped me was pre-deciding. I don't leave willingness up to chance in the moment. Sunday night, I decide when I'm working out that week. Not if—when. When

Monday morning rolls around and every part of me wants to stay in bed, I'm not making a decision. I'm just executing the decision I already made.

The next time you have to drive somewhere, turn your car into a classroom. On your next commute, check out the Huberman Lab podcast interview with Michael Easter, "Grow From Doing Hard Things." It is relevant and well done.

The Paradox of Willingness

The stuff you resist most often contains what you need most for your growth and fulfillment. I've seen this pattern over and over—in my own life and in the men I work with. That conversation you're avoiding? It's the gateway to deeper intimacy. That project you keep putting off? It's connected to your purpose. That physical challenge you're scared of? It's where you'll discover capacities you didn't know you had.

When I made that first jump out of the plane—remember that story from the First Heroic Dimension: Identity?—I was incongruent as hell. Terrified. But you know what happened? I hurled myself out of that bird anyway. And on that fifth jump, everything had changed. Not because I felt different, but because I'd been willing when I was feeling extremely unwilling.

Every time you choose willingness over comfort, you build self-trust and self-leadership. You're proving to yourself that your word means something, that you can count on yourself. And that changes everything.

Execution and Willingness

In the last dimension, we talked about execution—the systems, frameworks, and practical infrastructure for getting things done. That's the external architecture of action. It's essential. You need it.

Willingness is what happens in the split second before you engage those systems. It's the internal choice that activates everything else.

You can have the perfect morning routine designed—clothes laid out, coffee prepped, calendar blocked. That's execution. But when it's still dark outside, and your alarm goes off in the morning, there's still a moment where you choose. That moment is willingness.

Execution answers, "How do I do this consistently?" Willingness answers, "Will I do this right now when I really don't want to?"

Both are necessary. Neither is sufficient alone. You need the systems and the willingness to engage them.

When Willingness Is Hardest

Recognizing these moments helps you prepare for them.

- When you're already depleted. End of a long day, end of a hard week, when you've given everything, and there's one more thing that needs doing. This is when your willingness reserves are lowest. This is also when it matters most.
- When nobody's watching. It's easier to be willing when there's external accountability. But the character-defining moments happen when it's just you and the choice. No one would know if you skipped it. That's when you find out who you actually are.
- When the payoff is distant. Willingness is easier when the reward is immediate. But transformation requires being willing to do things whose benefits won't show up for months or years. That delayed gratification is brutal for our instant-gratification-wired brains.
- When you're winning. Counterintuitive, right? But I've

watched more guys lose willingness after initial success than after failure. Success breeds comfort. Comfort breeds complacency. Suddenly, you're coasting instead of climbing, and for some people, that's where willingness atrophies.

- When it contradicts your self-image. Maybe you see yourself as someone who doesn't ask for help, but willingness requires admitting you need support. Maybe you see yourself as independent, but willingness requires accepting that you're interdependent. The actions that challenge your identity are the hardest to be willing to do.

Willingness and Identity

Every act of willingness is an identity statement.

When you're willing to do the hard thing, you're declaring, "I'm the kind of person who keeps commitments to himself." When you're willing to face discomfort, you're declaring, "I'm the kind of person who values growth over comfort." When you're willing to begin before you're ready, you're declaring, "I'm the kind of person who acts despite fear."

And willingness that contradicts everything you were conditioned and trained to be is the hardest willingness of all. That's why willingness connects directly back to the First Heroic Dimension: Identity. Remember those parts we talked about—the conditioned self, the protective parts, the authentic self underneath?

Willingness is how you express your authentic self instead of defaulting to your conditioning.

Your conditioning wants comfort, safety, the familiar. Your authentic self wants growth, meaning, and transformation. Willingness is the bridge between those two.

Every time you choose willingness, you're strengthening the neural pathways of your authentic identity. You're literally

THE NINTH HEROIC DIMENSION: WILLINGNESS

rewiring your brain to default to action instead of avoidance, to engagement instead of retreat, to growth instead of comfort.

And willingness gets easier with practice. Not because the challenges get smaller, but because your capacity gets larger.

Practicing Willingness

Like the other heroic dimensions, willingness isn't a one-time decision. It's a practice you engage in multiple times every single day.

- Physical willingness: Moving your body when it wants to be still.
- Emotional willingness: Feeling what you'd rather avoid.
- Relational willingness: having the conversation you'd rather postpone.
- Creative willingness: Starting before you feel ready.
- Spiritual willingness: Sitting in silence when your mind wants distraction.

Each of these is a small act of willingness. Individually, they might not seem significant, but accumulated over days, weeks, and months, they become the difference between the life you're living and the life you're capable of.

I track my willingness. Not obsessively, but consciously. At the end of each day, I ask myself: "Where was I willing today when it would've been easier to be unwilling?" That question keeps me honest. It also shows me my patterns, like where my willingness is getting stronger and where it's weak.

But remember: progress, not perfection. Give yourself a break when you are gaining momentum. It's okay to indulge yourself in some comforts because we need these moments to appreciate our progress. But don't stay in the comfort bubble too long, because this can turn into forms of avoidance and resistance once again. Guard your comfort time for when it feels right.

When Unwillingness Might Be Wisdom

Sometimes, unwillingness is trying to tell you something legitimate.

If you're consistently unwilling to pursue a particular path, it might be a sign of misalignment. Maybe that vision isn't actually yours. Maybe it violates your values. Maybe it's someone else's dream you've been carrying.

The key is learning to distinguish between resistance that's protecting your comfort zone and resistance that's protecting your authentic self.

One way to tell the difference: Comfort-zone resistance feels like fear and avoidance. It comes with excuses and rationalizations. It wants you to stay small.

Authentic resistance feels different. It comes with clarity. It might say, "This isn't right for you," not "You can't do this." It protects your integrity, not an inflated ego.

When you feel unwillingness, pause and ask, "Is this protecting me from growth, or is this protecting me from something that doesn't align with who I am?" Be honest because the answer tells you whether to push through or course-correct.

The Compounding Effect of Willingness

Remember the compound effect we talked about in the Execution dimension and how small, consistent actions over time produce remarkable results? The same principle applies to willingness, maybe even more powerfully.

Every act of willingness makes the next one slightly easier. Not dramatically easier—you don't suddenly love doing hard things (that's why they're hard). But you build evidence for yourself. You prove that you can be willing when you're unwilling. You demonstrate that you survive discomfort. You show yourself that action creates the feeling, not the other way around.

This is how men transform. It's not through one heroic act of willingness, but through thousands of small ones. The guy who's willing to get out of bed when he doesn't feel like it, who's willing to have a difficult conversation, who's willing to start before he's ready, who's willing to keep going when results aren't immediately visible—that guy changes his life.

Willingness isn't just about the action you take. It's about the man you become through consistently choosing action over avoidance.

Willingness as the Activating Force

Let me bring this full circle by showing you how willingness activates every other dimension we've covered:

- Identity requires the willingness to face uncomfortable truths about who you've been and who you're becoming. Without willingness, you stay comfortable with your conditioned self.
- Values require the willingness to make difficult choices that honor what matters most. Without willingness, you compromise on what you claim to value.
- Meaning requires the willingness to transform your pain into purpose. Without willingness, suffering stays suffering.
- Purpose requires the willingness to pursue what you're here to contribute even when the path is unclear. Without willingness, purpose stays theoretical.
- Self-Care requires the willingness to prioritize your

well-being even when everything else feels more urgent. Without willingness, you deplete yourself.

- Roles require the willingness to show up intentionally in each important area of your life. Without willingness, you fragment.
- Vision requires the willingness to build toward a future you can't yet see. Without willingness, vision is just fantasy.
- Execution requires the willingness to engage your systems consistently. Without willingness, the best frameworks in the world sit unused.

Do you see it? Willingness is the catalyst. It's the spark that ignites everything else. All the clarity, all the frameworks, all the insights—they become transformative only through your willingness to act on them.

The Moment of Choice

Every day, multiple times a day, you face moments of choice. They're small moments, usually, and pretty unremarkable to anyone watching. But these moments are where transformation actually happens.

The alarm goes off. Do you get up or hit snooze? There's the moment.

You know you should make that call. Do you pick up the phone or find another task? There's the moment.

You're about to say something dishonest to avoid conflict. Do you speak your truth or stay comfortable? There's the moment.

Your workout is scheduled, and you had a long day at work. Do you go or rationalize skipping? There's the moment.

THE NINTH HEROIC DIMENSION: WILLINGNESS

These moments don't feel significant in isolation, but your life is the accumulated result of how you've handled thousands of these moments. Your future will be determined by how you handle the next thousand.

Willingness is what you choose in those moments. Not motivation. Not inspiration. Not feeling ready. Willingness. The simple, unglamorous choice to do what you said you'd do, to be who you said you'd be, to keep the commitment you made to yourself.

That's how heroes are made. Not in dramatic, public moments of glory, but in private moments of choice when nobody's watching, and nothing requires you to be willing except your own integrity.

Once you've built willingness in one area, you can apply it anywhere. Willingness is a transferable skill. The guy who learns to be willing to work out when he doesn't feel like it discovers he can also be willing to have difficult conversations, to start that business, to make that change he's been avoiding.

Willingness is the muscle that makes everything else possible. And like any muscle, it gets stronger through use.

INNER WORK SECTION

NOTES

THE WORK (Grab your journal!)

Time to get real about where unwillingness is blocking you and build your willingness practice.

1. Name what you're avoiding. What's the one thing you know you need to do, but you've been unwilling to start? Not a list of ten things—just one. The one that, if you handled it, would create the most significant positive change in your life right now. Write it down.

2. Identify your specific resistance pattern. When you think about doing that thing, what form does your resistance take? Review the three traps and be honest about which one you default to:
   a. Comfort Trap: "It's easier to stay where I am."
   b. Perfectionist's Paralysis: "I can't start until everything's perfect."
   c. Emotional Hostage: "I'll do it when I feel ready, motivated, or inspired."

3. Trace the cost. What has your unwillingness already cost you? Not in vague terms, but specifically. Lost time? Compromised relationships? Diminished self-respect? Missed opportunities? Accumulated regret? Write it out. Let yourself feel the real cost of staying unwilling.

4. Connect to your why. Go back to your Meaning and Purpose from earlier dimensions. How does being willing in this specific area serve your larger purpose? How does it express your values? How does it move you toward your vision? Make the connection explicit.

5. Design your moment of choice. You know when you'll face the willingness decision. Tomorrow morning at 5 a.m. Tomorrow afternoon, when you should make that call. Tomorrow evening, when you need to have

that conversation. Describe the exact moment when willingness will be required.

6. Set your pre-decision. Right now, decide what you'll do in that moment. Not "I'll see how I feel." Decide now: "When that moment comes, I will [specific action]." Write it down as a commitment. Think of this as an intentional inoculation to deal with resistance.

7. Use the Five-Second Rule. When the moment comes and you feel resistance, count: Five. Four. Three. Two. One. Then move your body toward the action. Don't think. Don't negotiate. Just move. Commit to doing this for one week straight.

Don't forget to track your willingness. Each evening, write down one sentence: "Today I was willing when I [specific action]." Even if you weren't perfectly willing in all areas, identify where you showed up. This builds evidence of your growing capacity.

Notice the pattern. After one week of willingness practice, answer these questions:

1. What changed in how you relate to yourself?
2. What did you discover about your capacity?
3. Where did willingness start to feel slightly easier?
4. What's the next area where you need to apply willingness?

Finally, complete this statement: "I am willing to be the kind of person who _____." This isn't aspirational—this is declarative. Who are you willing to become through your consistent choices? Write it. Then live it.

Remember that willingness isn't about feeling ready. It's about acting anyway. The feeling follows the action, not the other way around.

THE NINTH HEROIC DIMENSION: WILLINGNESS

Don't negotiate with weakness.

Every time you choose willingness over comfort, you're building the life you actually want. You're saying, "I'm the kind of man who moves, not the kind of man who waits."

MEN HARVESTING WISDOM

THE TENTH HEROIC DIMENSION:

LEGACY

The imprint you leave behind on other people and the world

"Your legacy is every life you touch."
—Maya Angelou

When you're gone, what will remain?

Not your bank account or your title or your possessions. Those evaporate fast. I'm talking about the part of you that continues on in the people you influenced, the values you embodied, and the work you did that outlives you.

For many reasons, people tend to avoid considering their legacy. I get it. Thinking about legacy means thinking about death, and most of us would rather not. We tell ourselves we'll worry about legacy later, when we're old, when we've accomplished more, when we have something worth leaving behind.

The truth is, your legacy isn't something you create at the end of your life. It's something you're building right now, whether you're conscious of it or not. Every choice you make, every interaction you have, every value you demonstrate or violate—it's all part of what you'll leave behind.

Legacy is the tenth dimension because it integrates everything that came before it. But it's also the dimension that changes how you approach all the others. When you start thinking about what will outlive you, you stop wasting time on shit that doesn't matter.

What Legacy Actually Is

My son died when he was twenty-nine years old. But his legacy didn't die with him.

The initial framework we developed together during those late-night phone calls when he first came home from Afghanistan—identity, mission, meaning, purpose—became the foundation for everything I've built since. The four foundational elements he and I worked on evolved into these ten dimensions I'm sharing with you. The men I've worked with are part of Danny's legacy. This book you're reading exists because of him.

Legacy isn't about being famous or important or having your name on a building. That's ego, not legacy. They could rename the same building after someone else once you're gone. What really matters is this: Was anyone helped before they put your name on that building? What you did for that person, for those people, that's legacy.

Real legacy is simple and profound. It's the values you live by that others absorb and carry forward. It's the people whose lives change because they crossed paths with you. It's the work you do that continues serving others after you're gone. It's how the world is different—even in small, unglamorous ways—because you walked through it.

Your legacy doesn't require you to do something extraordinary. It requires you to do something meaningful, consistently, aligned with who you actually are. That matters. It makes an impact, and even if you never see it, it still matters.

Glad's Legacy

I remember opening the old suitcase my great-aunt Glad left behind after she passed. It was a battered, timeworn thing she had carried through more than one war zone. Inside it, beneath a few personal belongings, I found a copy of a book she had written, One Woman's War. Its pages were yellowed with age, corners softened, and the margins filled with her tiny, handwritten notes. Glad was one of the only Canadian correspondents in Paris when it fell to the Germans in 1940. She stood inside history as Europe fractured and fell to the Nazis and documented it with a steadiness that still humbles me.

As I held that suitcase and the book inside it, I realized how deeply her legacy had shaped my life long before I ever understood it. Her courage wasn't loud or dramatic—it was deliberate, disciplined, and unwavering. She walked toward truth, even when the world was falling apart around her.

That suitcase felt less like an object and more like a handoff—a quiet passing of the torch. Glad left behind a standard, not just a book in a suitcase, and that standard is:

Serve something larger than yourself.

Let your work outlive you.

Why Men Avoid Legacy Thinking

There are a few reasons I believe we resist thinking about legacy, and they're worth examining because the resistance itself is telling you something.

1. **Fear of mortality.** Thinking about what you'll leave behind means accepting that you won't be here forever. That's uncomfortable. Most of us have an abstract awareness that we'll die someday, but we don't actually sit with that reality. Legacy thinking forces you to.
2. **Feeling insignificant.** A lot of guys think, "I'm nobody. What legacy could I possibly have?" This is bullshit, but it's common bullshit. You don't need to be Martin Luther King Jr. or Alexander the Great to leave a legacy. You just need to live with intention and integrity in your corner of the world. If anything, think about what the future generations of your offspring or nieces and nephews will gain from what you can leave behind for them.
3. **Pressure to be perfect.** Some guys avoid legacy thinking because they're aware of their failures and mistakes. "How can I think about my legacy when I've fucked up so much?" Here's the thing: your legacy isn't about perfection. It's about what you did with your imperfection, how you learned, what you passed forward.
4. **Present-focused overwhelm.** This one comes up all the time: "I'm just trying to get through the week. I don't have time to think about legacy." And that's exactly why you need to think about it. Legacy consciousness changes how you spend your Tuesday afternoon. It clarifies what actually matters, so you stop wasting energy on what doesn't.

Avoiding legacy thinking doesn't protect you from anything. It just increases the odds that you'll reach the end of your life with regrets about how you spent it.

The Channels of Legacy

Your legacy operates through different channels. Understanding them helps you see where you're already building something that will outlast you, and where you might want to be more intentional.

Values Legacy

This is the most fundamental form. The values you embody get transmitted to others, often unconsciously. Your kids absorb how you handle adversity, how you treat people, and what you prioritize. Your colleagues notice what you tolerate and what you won't. Your friends see what you stand for.

Viktor Frankl wrote about our ultimate freedom being the choice of how we respond to circumstances. That choice—lived out consistently—becomes your values legacy. People remember not just what you said but how you showed up when things were hard.

The choice to turn pain into purpose is part of my values legacy. And every man who makes a similar choice after experiencing loss, that's the value continuing forward.

Relationship Legacy

You impact people directly through your relationships with them, like how you show up in marriage, friendships, mentorships, even brief encounters—all of it creates ripples.

My great-aunt Glad's legacy in my life was enormous. She believed in me when I didn't believe in myself. She challenged me. She showed me what courage looked like through her actions as a war correspondent. I never forgot her lessons, and those lessons have influenced how I show up for other people. That's her legacy, extending through me to people she never met.

Who are you showing up for? Whose life is different because you're in it? That's relationship legacy building in real time.

Creative Legacy

The work you create—whether it's art, writing, a business, a system, a method—can outlive you by decades.

That's creative legacy. It's building something designed to outlast you, something that continues serving its purpose independent of your presence.

Creative legacy can be as simple as documenting your insights so your kids or grandkids can learn from them. It can be mentoring someone in your field who'll carry forward your approach. It can be doing your work with enough care and excellence that it influences how others approach similar work.

Community Legacy

How you contribute to your community—however you define community—creates legacy. Maybe it's your neighborhood. Maybe it's your professional field. Maybe, like me, it's Veterans, men in crisis, or people facing the same struggle you've overcome.

For thirty years, twenty to thirty hours per week, I've volunteered and worked with at-risk Veterans and men facing transitions. That's my community legacy. Most legacy isn't built through dramatic gestures. It's built through consistent presence over time.

Environmental Legacy

How you interact with the physical world matters. The resources you consume or conserve, and the environment you leave for the next generation is also part of your legacy.

This one's harder for some people to wrap their heads around because the impact feels distant and abstract. But every choice you make about consumption, sustainability, stewardship of what you've been given—it adds up, and it's important to be conscious of what that legacy is.

Legacy as Daily Practice

Remember, as with every other heroic dimension, your legacy is something you create every single day through your choices.

Every morning, when you decide whether to follow through on your commitments or blow them off, you are either building or eroding your legacy.

Legacy consciousness is so powerful that it changes your relationship with time. Instead of asking "What do I feel like doing right now?" you start asking "What choice will I be proud of looking back? What choice serves something larger than my immediate comfort?"

As always, this is about being intentional, not perfect. It's about recognizing that your life is the accumulated result of thousands of small choices, and those choices either build toward something meaningful or they don't.

What Actually Gets Remembered

What gets remembered is almost never what people think will be remembered.

Outside of a funeral situation, in actual, daily life, nobody's going to go on about your big accomplishments, titles, how much money you made, or what awards you won. That stuff evaporates fast.

Like Maya Angelou said, "People will forget what you said. People will forget what you did. But people will never forget how you made them feel." They remember whether you showed up when things were hard. Whether your actions matched your words. Whether you were the same person in private as you were in public.

They remember the time you helped them without being asked. The conversation that changed their perspective. The moment you chose integrity over convenience. The way you handled adversity with grace. The values you wouldn't compromise on.

That's what legacy looks like.

The Shadow Side of Legacy

I need to talk about something uncomfortable: negative legacy.

We all leave one. The question is whether we're aware of it and working to minimize it.

Every pattern you don't break, you pass forward. Every wound you don't heal, you transmit. Every value you violate, you model as acceptable.

My father's violence was part of his legacy to me. That violence came from his father. It was a pattern that had been transmitted through generations until I made the conscious choice to break it. It took decades of work to ensure I wouldn't pass that legacy to the next generation.

What negative patterns are you carrying that you haven't addressed? What dysfunction are you normalizing? What values are you violating that others are absorbing as acceptable?

Don't fall into a shame spiral here. This is the importance and imperative of awareness. Once you're conscious of the shadow side of your legacy, you can do something about it—but you can't change what you won't acknowledge.

How Legacy Integrates Everything

Legacy is the tenth dimension because it integrates all nine previous dimensions and transforms how you approach each one:

- **Identity:** When you think about legacy, you get clearer about who you actually are versus who you've been performing. Your authentic identity is what creates lasting impact.
- **Values:** Legacy clarifies which values are non-negotiable because you're thinking about what you want to pass forward, not just what feels comfortable now.
- **Meaning:** Your sense of meaning deepens when connected to impact beyond yourself. Suffering becomes more bearable when transformed into legacy.
- **Purpose:** Legacy extends your purpose beyond your lifetime. You're not just doing something meaningful—you're building something that continues.
- **Self-Care:** Legacy consciousness makes self-care essential, not optional. You can't build a lasting legacy if you burn out or destroy yourself in the process.
- **Roles:** Legacy helps you see how your various roles connect to something larger. You're not just a father—you're shaping the next generation.

- **Vision:** Your vision becomes more compelling when connected to legacy. You're not just building a life—you're building something that outlasts you.
- **Execution:** Legacy focuses your execution on what actually matters long-term, not just what's urgent right now.
- **Willingness:** Legacy provides the "why" that makes willingness easier. When you're building something that outlives you, temporary discomfort matters less.

It all connects. Each dimension supports the next, and legacy is where they all come together and point beyond yourself.

Living Your Legacy Now

I want to close this dimension with something practical because legacy thinking can get abstract fast.

Your legacy has already begun. Honing and reforging it begins today.

The way you show up in the next conversation you have—that's legacy.

The choice you make about how to spend the next hour—that's legacy.

The value you demonstrate or violate in the next decision—that's legacy.

You don't need permission to start building a meaningful legacy. You don't need to wait until you've accomplished more or become more or fixed all your shit. You start from where you are with what you have.

After Danny passed, I didn't have some grand plan for how to turn my grief into legacy. I just started showing up for other men who were struggling. My legacy was built one conversation at a time, one framework at a time, one moment at a time.

Decades later, that's become something larger than I could have imagined. As I explained in the Fourth Heroic Dimension: Purpose, it's not because I was special or talented or had some unique advantage, but because I kept showing up, kept refining, kept serving. Consistency over time creates legacy.

You can do the same. You don't need a foundation or a book or a platform—even if you might one day. No matter what you do, you just need to live your values consistently, show up for people authentically, do work that matters, and keep choosing integrity over comfort.

That's how legacy gets built: through thousands of small choices aligned with something larger than yourself.

When you start living with legacy consciousness, your life becomes richer. You stop wasting time on petty things. You stop seeking approval from people who don't matter. You stop compromising on what's actually important.

Are You Proud of Your Legacy?

If you died tomorrow, would you be proud of the legacy you're leaving?

That question cuts through all the bullshit fast. It clarifies what needs to change and what needs to stay. It separates the essential from the trivial.

You don't need to have the perfect answer to that question right now. But you need to ask it. Regularly. Because that question keeps you honest about whether your life matches your stated values, whether your choices align with your purpose, and whether you're building something worth leaving behind.

Legacy isn't created by men who wait for inspiration. Legacy is created by men who act. Men who choose the hard thing. Men who stop negotiating with their comfort and step into the life they know they're here to live.

From here on out, every choice you make is either reinforcing your legacy or eroding it.

Your legacy is your marching orders.

Stand up.

Step in.

Build what only you can build.

INNER WORK SECTION

NOTES

THE WORK (Grab your journal!)

This is it—the final dimension, where everything comes together. Take your time with this work.

Write your legacy statement. Imagine it's fifty or more years from now. You're gone. Someone who knew you well is describing your life and impact to someone who never met you. What do you hope they would say? Write out:

- The values you embodied consistently
- The impact you had on specific people or communities
- What continued after you were gone because of how you lived

Assess your current trajectory. Now be brutally honest: if you died tomorrow, would the legacy you're actually building match the legacy statement you just wrote? Where's the gap? What are you doing that serves your desired legacy? What are you doing that contradicts it?

Identify your legacy channels. For each channel, write one specific way you're building (or want to build) legacy:

- **Values Legacy:** What value do you want to be known for? How are you demonstrating this in your everyday life?
- **Relationship Legacy:** Who are you showing up for consistently? Whose life is better because you're in it?
- **Creative Legacy:** What are you creating that could serve others after you're gone?
- **Community Legacy:** How are you contributing to something larger than yourself?
- **Environmental Legacy:** What are you stewarding for the next generation?

Name your shadow legacy. What negative patterns are you carrying that you haven't addressed? What dysfunction are you normalizing? What would you not want to pass forward?

Write it down. Then write: "To break this pattern, I commit to _____."

Set your legacy intention for this week. Based on everything you've written, complete this sentence: "This week, to honor the legacy I want to create, I will _____." Make it concrete and measurable. Do it. Then next week, do it again.

Review the ten dimensions. You've worked through all ten dimensions now. Go back and look at your work from each one:

1. **Identity:** Who are you beneath the conditioning?
2. **Values:** What principles guide your life?
3. **Meaning:** Why does your life matter?
4. **Purpose:** How do you express your meaning?
5. **Self-Care:** How do you maintain your capacity?
6. **Roles:** How do you organize your important areas?
7. **Vision:** What future are you building?
8. **Execution:** How do you make it real?
9. **Willingness:** Will you act when it's hard?
10. **Legacy:** What will outlive you?

Write out how all ten dimensions connect in your life. How does your identity inform your values? How do your values create meaning? How does meaning point to purpose? How does purpose require self-care? How do your roles express your purpose? How does your vision extend beyond your lifetime? How does execution make it real? How does willingness activate everything? How does legacy integrate it all?

Make your commitment. This is the culmination of all the work you've done. Complete this statement:

"I commit to building a legacy defined by _____. I will do this by showing up consistently in these ways: _____.

THE TENTH HEROIC DIMENSION: LEGACY

I understand that my legacy is being created now, not later, and that every choice matters. I choose to live with intention and integrity, aligned with my authentic self and values, in service of something larger than my immediate comfort. This is my path forward."

Sign it. Date it. This is your declaration of transformational self-leadership.

MEN HARVESTING WISDOM

TRIANGULATION FOR MANAGING CHANGE AND TRANSITION:

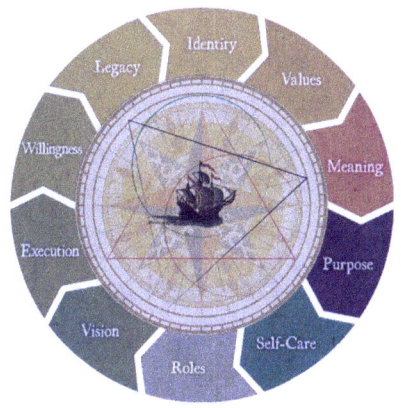

How to Use the Ten Heroic Dimensions Simultaneously

How to find yourself when life knocks the compass out of your hands

> "Everyone has his or her own way of learning things... His way isn't the same as mine, nor mine as his. But we're both in search of our Personal Legends, and I respect him for that."
> — Paulo Coelho, *The Alchemist*

When you're hiking in unfamiliar terrain and realize you've lost the trail, you don't just pick a random direction and hope for the best. You stop. You look around. You identify multiple landmarks—a distant peak, a river, a ridge line—and you use those reference points together to triangulate your position.

That's exactly how these ten dimensions work when you're facing a major life transition or crisis.

You don't need to work on all ten dimensions at once—as I've said before, that's a recipe for overwhelm. But the Ten Heroic Dimensions all build off one another and work together. That's why a powerful transformation happens when you identify which two to three dimensions are most relevant to your specific situation and use them together as navigation points.

This is the practical application of everything we've covered. Here's how to use the framework when your life gets disrupted.

The Principle of Triangulation

In navigation, triangulation is the process of determining your position by measuring angles to three known points. The more reference points you have, the more accurately you can pinpoint where you are and chart a course forward.

The Ten Heroic Dimensions work the same way. When you're in crisis or transition, you're often disoriented. You can't see clearly. You don't know which way is forward. But if you can identify which dimensions are most relevant to your situation, you suddenly have reference points. You can figure out where you are and what needs your attention.

Triangulation Checklist

Answer these questions when you're disoriented or unsure where to begin:

1. What transition am I in right now? Identity shift, overwhelm, drifting, mortality, execution gap, etc.
2. What is my current emotional state? Lost? Numb? Angry? Exhausted? Scared?
3. Which two to three dimensions match this situation? Identity + Values + Purpose? Self-Care + Roles + Execution?

4. What's the next right question I need to answer? Who am I now? What matters? What do I need? What do I fear?
5. What's the next right action I can take this week? Something small, specific, and actionable.

The dimensions you focus on aren't determined by your age or your achievements or where you "should" be in life. They're determined by the specific challenge you're facing right now.

A twenty-five-year-old might need to focus on legacy and meaning if he's facing a terminal diagnosis. A sixty-year-old might need identity and purpose if he just got laid off after thirty years with the same company. The framework adapts to your situation, not to some arbitrary life stage.

Let me show you how this works across common transitions and crises men face.

INNER WORK SECTION

NOTES

THE WORK (Grab your journal!)

When Your Identity Gets Stripped Away

The Situation: Job loss. Military transition. Divorce. Forced retirement. Empty nest. Any moment when the primary identity you've built your life around suddenly disappears.

Primary Dimensions to Navigate By:

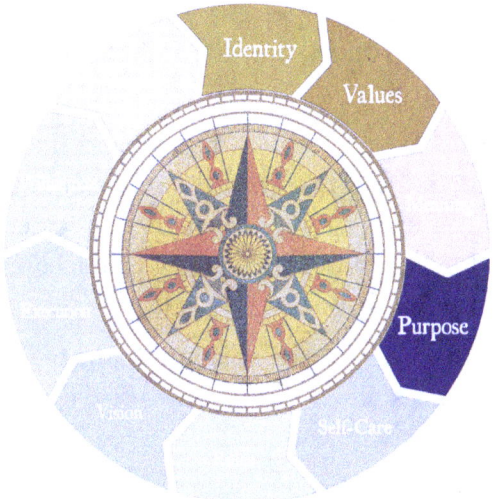

- **Identity:** Who am I without this role?
- **Values:** What actually matters to me beneath the performance?
- **Purpose:** How will I contribute now?

Why These Three Work Together:

When your primary identity collapses, you're facing the most fundamental question a man can ask: "Who the hell am I without the thing that defined me?"

This is exactly where Danny was when he called me from that frozen ditch. The uniform was gone. The rank was gone.

The mission was gone. The men he led were gone. He had no idea who he was without those external markers.

We started with identity. Who was he before the Army shaped him? What parts of himself had he suppressed to fit the military mold? What was authentic versus conditioned?

From there, values became the compass. What mattered to him beyond the mission? What principles would guide him now that he didn't have orders to follow? Turned out, service and brotherhood weren't just military values—they were Danny's core values that the military had given him a structure to express.

That clarity led to purpose: How could he express those values in civilian life? How could he serve and build brotherhood without a uniform? That's when he decided to become a counselor for Veterans. New identity, same core values, new expression of purpose.

This is the power of triangulation. Identity alone left him feeling lost. Values alone felt abstract. Purpose alone had no foundation. But when he used all three together as navigation points, he could chart a course forward.

If you're in an identity crisis right now, answer these three questions:

1. Who am I when no one is watching and nothing is required of me? (Identity)
2. What principles would I defend even if it costs me something? (Values)
3. How could I serve others in a way that expresses who I actually am? (Purpose)

Write your answers. Look for where they overlap. That's your path forward.

When You're Overwhelmed and Running on Empty

The Situation: New parenthood. Caregiving for aging parents. Career pressure with no end in sight. Multiple competing demands that leave you depleted, fragmented, and questioning how long you can sustain this pace.

Primary Dimensions to Navigate By:

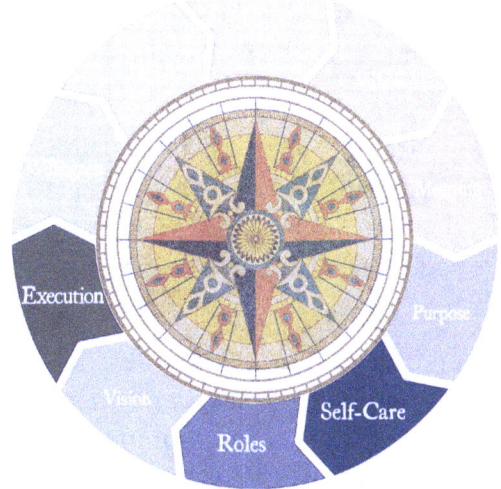

- **Self-Care:** Am I maintaining my capacity?
- **Roles:** How am I showing up in each area?
- **Execution:** What systems support consistency?

Why These Three Work Together:

When you're overwhelmed, your instinct is to push harder, do more, sleep less, and just power through. That works for a while. Then it destroys you.

I've watched men—myself included—sacrifice their health, their relationships, and their sanity trying to meet every obligation without ever asking whether the way they're organized is sustainable.

This is where self-care, roles, and execution create a system that actually works.

Self-care forces the question: "What do I need to maintain my physical, emotional, spiritual, and financial capacity for the long haul?" Not "what would be nice"—what's non-negotiable for you to keep functioning?

For me, that's exercise, sleep, and time with guys who need and understand this work. Yours might be different, but you need to know what they are.

Roles bring clarity to how you're actually spending your energy. When you map out your key roles—father, husband, professional, whatever—you can see where you're overextended and where you're neglecting what matters. You can set clear intentions for how you want to show up instead of just reacting to whoever's loudest.

Execution is where you build systems that make all of this sustainable. You can't rely on motivation or willpower when you're already depleted. Like William Sprague said, "Do not wait to strike till the iron is hot; but make it hot by striking." You need structures that work whether you feel like it or not. Morning routines. Weekly planning sessions. Boundaries around work hours. Whatever makes your self-care and your role intentions actually happen consistently.

Together, these three dimensions create sustainability. Self-care without execution becomes aspirational bullshit you never actually do. Roles without self-care lead to burnout. Execution without clear roles just makes you "efficiently" exhausted.

THE WORK

If you're running on empty right now, do this:

TRIANGULATION FOR MANAGING CHANGE AND TRANSITION

1. List your non-negotiable self-care requirements (be honest, not aspirational).
2. Identify your three to five most important roles and write one intention for how you want to show up in each.
3. Design one system this week that supports both your self-care and your role intentions.

When You're Drifting Without Direction

The Situation: You're functional, maybe even successful, but something's missing. You're going through the motions but can't shake the feeling that you're drifting instead of building something that matters. You're busy as hell but not sure what any of it's for.

Primary Dimensions to Navigate By:

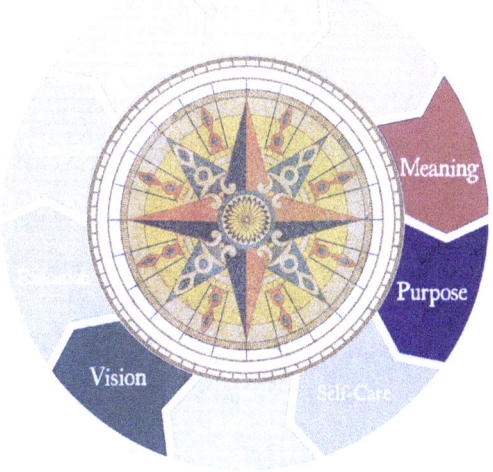

- **Meaning:** Why does my life matter?
- **Purpose:** How do I express that meaning?
- **Vision:** What future am I building toward?

Why These Three Work Together:

Drifting is a special kind of hell because everything looks fine from the outside. People wouldn't describe you as "in crisis." You're not failing. You're just...empty. Numb. Going through the motions.

I once worked with a man who had everything most people chase—money, success, a respected position—yet he told me he felt like a ghost living someone else's life. He was drifting. He showed up to every meeting with the same hollow look in his eyes and finally said, "I'm doing everything right, but nothing feels meaningful anymore." It wasn't until he reconnected with what gave his life meaning that he finally could see a future worth moving toward. His external success had nothing to do with it—his internal alignment did.

Viktor Frankl wrote that man's primary motivation is the search for meaning. When meaning is absent, everything feels hollow, no matter how successful you are externally.

This is where meaning, purpose, and vision create forward momentum.

Meaning answers the existential question: "Why am I here? What's my life actually for?" This isn't about some grand, fanciful destiny. It's about what gives your specific existence significance. For me, it's helping men who are struggling. For you, it might be something completely different. But until you can answer that question with clarity, you'll drift.

Purpose takes your meaning and makes it concrete: "How do I actually live this out? What's my specific contribution?" As I've said before, meaning is the why, purpose is the how. They work together—meaning without purpose stays theoretical, and purpose without meaning feels arbitrary.

Vision is where you create a compelling picture of the future that organizes your present choices. You're not just understanding your meaning or knowing your purpose—you're building toward something specific that expresses both. Vision pulls you forward instead of you having to push yourself.

When I lost my vision completely during those dark weeks of doomscrolling, it wasn't until I reconnected to my meaning (helping men who are suffering) that I could see my purpose again (building frameworks and sitting with guys in crisis) and that led to a renewed vision (this work continuing long after I'm gone, helping men I'll never meet).

THE WORK

If you're drifting right now, answer these:

1. What would make my suffering worthwhile? What cause is worth my pain? (Meaning)
2. What contribution could I make that only I can make with my specific experiences and skills? (Purpose)
3. What future, if I could see it clearly, would make me willing to endure the difficulty of getting there? (Vision)

Write until you have clarity. Don't settle for generic answers.

When You Face Your Mortality

The Situation: Health crisis. The death of someone close. A near-miss accident. Any moment when you're forced to confront the fact that your time is limited and you won't be here forever.

Primary Dimensions to Navigate By:

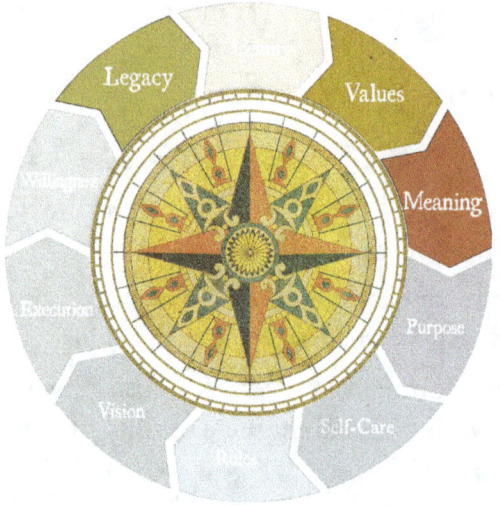

- **Meaning:** Has my life mattered?
- **Legacy:** What will remain after I'm gone?
- **Values:** Am I living according to what I claim matters most?

Why These Three Work Together:

Nothing clarifies what matters like facing death—yours or someone you love.

When Danny passed, I had to confront the brutal question: "What remains now that he's gone?"

The only answer that made his death even remotely bearable was meaning. His struggle wasn't for nothing. The work we did together, the framework we built, the late-night conversations—all of it could continue serving other men. His life mattered because it created meaning that outlasted him.

That's when legacy became real for me. Not as an abstract concept I'd think about when I was old, but as something being built right now through my daily choices. Every guy I sit with, every framework I refine, every conversation I have—that's Danny's legacy at work. That's my legacy being built.

But legacy without values is just ego. It's wanting to be remembered without actually living according to what you claim matters. So values become your test: Am I actually living aligned with what I say matters most? Or am I just performing for an imagined audience?

Meaning gives you the "why your life matters." Legacy shows you "what will remain." Values ensure "you're living it now, not just talking about it."

After losing Danny, I could have retreated into bitterness. That wouldn't have violated my stated values because I'd never examined them closely. But when I got clear that service and helping men in crisis were core values for me, suddenly retreating wasn't an option. My choices had to align with my values if I wanted to build a legacy that mattered.

THE WORK

If you're confronting mortality—yours or someone else's—sit with these questions:

1. Has my life mattered? How? (Meaning)
2. What will remain after I'm gone because of how I lived? (Legacy)
3. Are my daily choices aligned with what I claim matters most? (Values)

Don't rush this. These are the questions that clarify everything else.

When You Know What to Do But Can't Make Yourself Do It

The Situation: You've done the internal work. You have clarity on who you are, what matters, and where you're going, but you can't seem to translate that clarity into consistent action. You're stuck in the gap between knowing and doing.

Primary Dimensions to Navigate By:

- **Execution:** What systems support consistent action?
- **Willingness:** Will I act when I don't feel like it?
- **Self-Care:** Do I have the capacity to sustain this?

Why These Three Work Together:

It's not uncommon to get stuck here. That's why execution is about building systems that work whether you're motivated or not. Daily routines and weekly planning. Environmental design that makes the right choice easier and the wrong choice harder. You need infrastructure for consistency.

But systems aren't enough. Like we discussed in the Ninth Heroic Dimension: Willingness, there's always that moment—when the alarm goes off, when you need to have a hard conversation, when you should do the thing but every part of you resists—where willingness matters more than any system. Willingness is the choice to act when everything in you says not to.

And both execution and willingness require self-care. You can't build sustainable systems if you're depleted. You can't access willingness when your tank is empty. The guy who's chronically exhausted, emotionally dysregulated, and running on fumes can't execute consistently no matter how good his systems are.

This triangle creates sustainable transformation. Execution without willingness means you've got great plans you never follow through on. Willingness without execution means you're just white-knuckling your way forward with no structure, and without self-care, you'll burn out before you build anything lasting.

THE WORK

If you're stuck in the knowing-doing gap:
1. Design one execution system for your most important behavior. Be specific.
2. Identify the moment where willingness will be required tomorrow, like what time, what situation.
3. Assess honestly: Do you have the physical, emotional, and mental capacity to sustain this? If not, what element of your self-care needs attention first?

Using the Ten Heroic Dimensions As You Navigate

I want to be clear here: These aren't the only combinations that work. These are just examples. You might face a situation that requires a different set of dimensions working together. The point is to identify which dimensions are most relevant to your specific challenge right now and use them together as navigation points.

So, I'll say it again:

When you're disoriented, when you've lost the trail, when you don't know which way is forward—stop. Look around. Identify your landmarks. Use them together to figure out where you are and chart your course.

That's how you navigate from breakdown to breakthrough.

That's how you lead yourself through transformation.

That's how you become the hero of your own journey.

THE WORK

Your Current Transition

Describe the transition or challenge you're facing right now in detail. Not "life is hard" but "I just got laid off after fifteen years" or "my marriage is falling apart" or "I'm taking care of my dying father while trying to be present for my kids."

Your Navigation Points

Looking at the transition types described in this chapter, which one most closely matches your situation? Which two to three dimensions would serve as the most useful navigation points for where you are right now?

Don't overthink this. Your instinct is usually right. Which dimensions, if you got clear on them, would give you the most traction?

Your Immediate Action

For each of the two to three dimensions you identified, complete this sentence:

"To navigate my current situation, I need to get clear on ___(dimension)___. The one question I need to answer is _____. This week, I will take one action toward that clarity by _____."

Be specific. Make it doable. Put it on your calendar.

MEN HARVESTING WISDOM

CONCLUSION:

COMMITTING TO HEROIC SELF-LEADERSHIP

"Inaction breeds doubt and fear. Action breeds confidence and courage."

—Dale Carnegie

Calculate how many weeks you have left.

There are fifty-two weeks in a year. Let's say you live to ninety. That's 4,680 weeks total.

Now subtract your current age.

I'm sixty-four. That means I've already used 3,276 weeks, leaving me with roughly 1,404 weeks remaining.

When you think of your life in weeks instead of years, time starts to feel more urgent, more precious, more real.

I don't share this to depress you. I share it because knowing my time horizon changed how I live. I see more, love more, give more of myself in service of others. Moments matter differently when you understand how finite they are.

Throughout my day, I now ask myself what I will accomplish this week. That urgency has made me more intentional about everything—the relationships I invest in, the work I pursue, the legacy I'm building. It's clarified what matters and what doesn't. It's informed how I do the work with my personal Ten Heroic Dimensions.

So, do the math. Write down your number. Let it settle in.

Consider what you're going to do with the weeks you have left.

You've journeyed through ten dimensions now. Ten essential aspects of knowing yourself and leading yourself toward the life you actually want to live.

I'll leave you with the same question I ask the men I work with:

Who are you becoming?

This is your hero's journey. Not the mythical kind—the real kind. It doesn't mean you're going to save the world or get a medal. Heroic, transformational self-leadership means you face the parts of yourself most people run from—the parts you've been running from. It means you do the hard internal work that has no audience, no applause, no external validation.

It means you commit to:

1. **Identity:** Know who you are beneath the conditioning, the masks, and the protective parts you've built, and live from your authentic self instead of performing for approval.

2. **Values:** Clarify what actually matters to you and make

CONCLUSION: COMMITTING TO HEROIC SELF-LEADERSHIP

choices aligned with those values, even when it costs you something.

3. **Meaning:** Understand what gives your life significance and transform your suffering into something that serves others.

4. **Purpose:** Discover your unique contribution and pursue it consistently, not just when it's convenient.

5. **Self-Care:** Maintain yourself physically, emotionally, spiritually, and financially so you have the capacity to do what matters most.

6. **Roles:** Show up fully in your most important roles with clear intentions about who you're being, not just what you're doing.

7. **Vision:** Build a compelling future that's worth the struggle of getting there, and let that vision organize your daily choices.

8. **Execution:** Create systems that work whether you're motivated or not, and follow through on what you said you'd do.

9. **Willingness:** Act when everything in you resists, choosing growth over comfort in the moments that actually matter.

10. **Legacy:** Live each day knowing that what you do now shapes what remains after you're gone.

That's heroic, not because it's dramatic, but because it's hard. Because most people won't do it. What separates men who transform from men who stay stuck isn't perfection; it's persistence. It's showing up for yourself consistently, even when it's hard, even when progress feels slow, even when you'd rather not.

But you're here. You've read this far. You know something in your life needs to change. That matters.

That's why this isn't an ending. It's a beginning.

Remember that you are not your experiences, but all the experiences you've had and all the experiences you've avoided have shaped your perception and worldview. The fundamental distinction between being and experiencing creates the space for actual growth. Our experiences influence and the environments we create around us powerfully, positive and negative, for better and for worse, but they are not us. You are not what you do for a living. You are not even your thoughts—you are the observer of those thoughts. You have the capacity for agency and choice, so be mindful of what you tell yourself. When self-talk gets negative, take a step back and remember to observe.

Remember, the Ten Heroic Dimensions aren't meant to be worked through once and forgotten. They're a framework you return to throughout your life, particularly during times of change, transitions, and crises. Your understanding of each dimension will deepen over time. Your answers will evolve. That's how it's supposed to work.

Now, you have a choice. You can let this book gather dust on your shelf, or you can use these ten dimensions as your operating system for transformational self-leadership.

Not tomorrow. Not when you're ready. Not when it's convenient.

Now.

So, are you going to lead yourself like your life depends on it?

Because it does.

It's time to show up as the man you're capable of being.

AFTERWORD

"The two most important days of your life are when you are born and when you find out why."

— Mark Twain

The people and experiences that have significantly influenced the creation of this body of work carry their own weight: the inspiring life of my son Danny, and his passing after returning from Afghanistan; the profound mentorship and influence of my great-aunt "Glad" Gladys; a lifelong inward journey to the transformative depths and heights of self-leadership; a myriad of existential crises that forced me to learn, grow, and evolve; and I am profoundly grateful for the mentors and helpers that appeared on my path just when I needed them.

The cathartic experience of writing and publishing my second book, Be the Dawn in the Darkness, was a crucible that transformed my deepest wounds into something meaningful and healing. That book told my story. The Ten Heroic Dimensions of Transformational Self-Leadership is my invitation to you—an opportunity to begin your own transformational growth and to harvest wisdom from your own life experiences.

Through this work, all under the Men Harvesting Wisdom umbrella, I discovered that while my past profoundly shaped me, it doesn't define me, and my past will not master me. Reducing and releasing the burdens of regret and shame has brought me liberation and vulnerability.

The remedy for living with trauma, anxiety, and depression is actively and relentlessly living a meaning-filled and purpose-filled life. A human being living without meaning and purpose is a stifled soul.

Every day, a small part of me tries to convince myself that I'm broken and unworthy. I spend the rest of my day convincing myself that I'm not and that I am. And whenever I have felt entirely inadequate to write and share this work, I recall a quote from Marianne Williamson: "Our deepest fear is not that we are inadequate. Our deepest fear is that we are powerful beyond measure."

Once again, I am so thankful for Steven Pressfield, author of The War of Art: Break Through the Blocks and Win Your Inner Creative Battles. This work helped me understand the many faces of resistance writers and artists experience when bringing their works from a vision into reality. I was not alone in the sleepless nights of doubting myself, despairing over making little progress that often stretched for weeks and months. It was helpful to hear Steven's message over and over as I listened to his audiobook repeatedly.

Had it not been for my relentless pursuit to become who I was meant to be by harvesting the wisdom from my life experiences, this book would still be a rambling list of hopeful ideas in my head, never to see the light of day.

To you, the reader, the listener, the guy doing the work: Perhaps there is an action or a work of art in you as well that you have been resisting until you are old enough, good enough, successful enough—which, of course, is bullshit. Your work could be in the form of writing a bestselling book, painting a masterpiece, living a dream, changing careers, or simply finding what brings you joy.

Like Tony Robbins says, "If you think you can't, then you must!"

AFTERWORD

If you had a terrible and challenging upbringing, this means you have the gift of empathy to understand the pain of others.

If you have lived in shame and regret, stop focusing on the images and home movies stuck in your head, and stop projecting them into your future. Take your power back from focusing on your pain and limitations, and focus on who you are becoming. If necessary, break off the rearview mirror in the forefront of your mind and throw it in the trash.

As the great philosopher Jim Rohn once said, "Your past is here to serve you, not to master you." There are countless reasons and rationalizations to keep ourselves small. Thank them for sharing, then shift the focus of your attention, taking one step at a time toward fulfilling your hopes and dreams.

Be a good example of what you can do with your life, no matter your circumstances or physical or emotional limitations, real or perceived. Your life matters. You are here for a purpose, and it is up to you to discover this for yourself. Be of service to others, create your masterpiece, and by all means, fulfill your life's purpose.

What remains is a profound realization you've probably heard from others: Your past is your past, the future hasn't happened yet, and all you truly have is this moment. Now, in the later season of my own life, moments matter differently. Food tastes better, and moments are more meaningful because I savor them.

If I could have provisioned myself early in life with some key insights and wisdom to aid me on my hero's journey, the short list would be as follows:

- Wisdom is the result of good judgment; good judgment is the result of experience; experience is the result of bad judgment. (Inspired by a Mark Twain quote.)

- The most universally potent and beneficial mantra for self-care and humility I have learned is: progress, not perfection.

- We are all here to learn, so be curious and apply everything to yourself first.

- Your greatest teachers will meet you at the end of your rope—don't give up.

- No gurus. Teachers fall from the pedestals we put them on, and even monkeys fall from trees.

- Your most treasured life lessons will take root in your greatest challenges and suffering. The learning is in the struggle.

- Do what you fear most.

- Tame your monkey mind. Its only job is to worry, doubt your potential, and keep you small.

- Nurture your rational, reasonable mind. It knows your highest good and what is best for you.

- Do whatever it takes to free your soul.

- Take new snapshots of yourself and others regularly to own and celebrate who you are becoming.

- Be the joy in everything.

- Be the dawn in the darkness.

AFTERWORD

May your suffering shape you, your wisdom guide you, and your courage carry you into the man you were meant to become.

Lastly, to get this work into your bones, share what you are learning with others:

Learn it, teach it, master it!

Welcome to the heroic journey of transformational self-leadership.

Now, go do the work.

—J.H. Parker, 2026

The End

J. H. PARKER

AUTHOR-BEHAVIORAL ASSESSMENT ANALYST, AUDIOBOOK PRODUCER/NARRATOR.
CREATOR OF:

The Ten Essential Dimensions of Transformational Self-Leadership

For over 35 years, I've immersed myself in the inner work of personal, professional, transformational, and spiritual growth with a practical philosophy:

- Teachers fall from the pedestals we put them on, and even monkeys fall from trees; I am not here to teach or preach to you because I am in this heroic journey of life with you, often times, failing forward.
- No gurus, we are all here to learn.
- Be a curious learner.
- Apply everything to self, first.
- Focus on progress, not perfection.
- Continuously cultivate Self-Leadership.
- The Learning Is In The Struggle

ALSO BY
J.H. PARKER

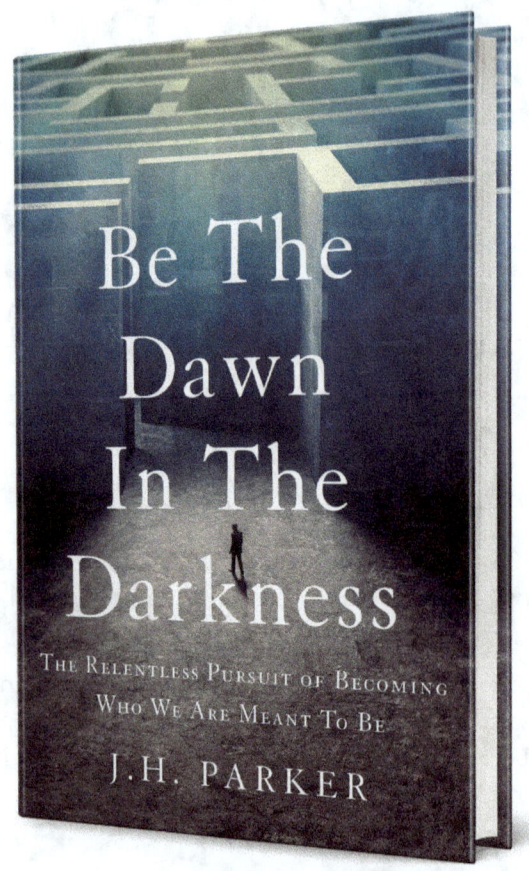

HarvestingWisdom.com

ALSO BY
J.H. PARKER

TransitioningVeteransBook.com

www.ingramcontent.com/pod-product-compliance
Lightning Source LLC
Chambersburg PA
CBHW071155070526
44584CB00019B/2799